100 ANSWERS
TO YOUR QUESTIONS ON
ANNULMENTS

EDWARD N. PETERS, J.D., J.C.D.

FOREWORD BY MOST REV. JOHN J. MYERS, J.D., J.C.D.

SIMON & SCHUSTER CUSTOM PUBLISHING

"The Magdalen Reading," by Rogier van der Weyden
Reproduced courtesy of the Trustees, The National Gallery, London.

Printed in the United States of America

10 9 8 7 6 5 4 3 2 1

ISBN 0-536-00172-3
BA 97321

SIMON & SCHUSTER CUSTOM PUBLISHING
160 Gould Street/Needham Heights, MA 02194
Simon & Schuster Education Group

Contents

Acknowledgments

Although the deficiencies in this book are entirely mine, its strengths draw from many sources. I am grateful to Drs. Robert Kennedy and Thomas Green of the Catholic University of America, who taught me how to read the Church's marriage law with precision and insight; to Msgr. Joseph Sadusky of the Archdiocese of Washington, who provided the best tribunal internship a student could hope to have; and to Bishop Roger Schwietz, OMI, and Fr. Dale Nau of the Diocese of Duluth, who first assigned me to tribunal duties and who patiently explained many things I should have already known. Most of all, though I am grateful to Bishop Robert Brom and to the entire staff of the Tribunal of the Diocese of San Diego who, along with the appellate judges of the Province of Los Angeles, make sure that I learn something new about marriage and ministry every day.

Ad Angelam Meam.

Foreword

The Sacrament of marriage is a holy institution, ordered to the good of the spouses and the procreation and education of children. In this life-giving sacramental relationship the couple establishes a partnership for the entire life. This partnership, once validly established and consummated between the couple, is unable to be dissolved by human power. This is the great strength of marriage, that it is a partnership in which the couple is joined and spiritually nourished by God. This truth also, however, means that marriage is a serious commitment, one that should not be entered lightly.

Sadly we know that through the centuries people have entered marriage without sufficient readiness. In addition there have always been impediments or other defects that have been understood to mar this commitment, and make a marriage a non-Sacramental one. Throughout the centuries the Church, in an expression of the mercy of Christ, has sought ways to investigate the possibility that a marriage might have been defective in its inception, and thus not be binding upon a person. Occasionally this has allowed a person to

marry again, permitting them to enter a valid sacramental union.

The legal process by which a former marriage has
been declared null has been described in various ways
through the centuries. For the last twenty years, or so,
the "annulment process" has been much in vogue in
the United States. Stemming from the great crisis of
divorce in our society, many Tribunals have seen an
explosion in the amount of people seeking declarations of nullity for former marriages. Many Tribunals
have responded, and from a desire to extend the
mercy of Christ to those in difficult situations, have
become more efficient. Almost all Tribunals have
staggered under the crunch. In many cases procedural
and other legal norms may not have been followed as
well as we might hope, and the parties involved did
not always understand the nature of the process they
were undertaking.

In recent years most tribunals have attempted to
stabilize their practice, and to conform their jurisprudence more closely with the practice of the Holy See.
This jurisprudence is expressed in the sentences of
the Roman Rota, the highest tribunal of the Universal
Church. This has led to a helpful clarification of just
legal norms, and a greater understanding of each
tribunal's role in the search for truth in the difficult
subject of marriages and annulments. Sadly, for some,
it has also led to confusion with the process. The
annulment that they sought was not so sure and
certain. The books they had read, and people they had
spoken to, had assured them that they just had to fill
out the papers. The annulment they expected was not
forthcoming.

This book will be helpful in filling a gap that has
existed for some time in literature dealing with annul-

ments. So many books have treated the legal process as merely a healing process, to assist the party to bring closure to a past marriage before embarking on another endeavor. Missing from many works was an honest explanation that not every process ends in an affirmative decision. The present work seems to be a balanced and helpful assessment of the annulment process. It will greatly aid people in understanding the process, and their options for proceeding in the case of a former marriage.

The format of this work is well suited to deal with specific questions which often surface in the process. The book is organized into various sections and questions, which may assist those who are confused by a particular aspect of the annulment process. Included is general information about the process and about the officials involved in the process. The information provided on the possible grounds for an annulment should help to clarify some questions for the reader. Often, people seeking annulments have complicated questions. A few typical ones are included by Dr. Peters. These questions will help the reader, proving to be a valuable resource for those who can identify their own situation in the examples given.

A few sections in particular should be highlighted as being highly valuable. Many works on annulments ignore the possibility that the process could end in a negative response. Dr. Peters includes insightful information for those who do receive a negative response. Inclusion of this material acknowledges the reality of the canonical process, prepares the reader for that possible outcome, and may assist those who are frustrated or dismayed after having received a negative sentence. Another valuable section includes questions for those who are not seeking an annulment, but who are nonetheless involved in the process. These include former spouses and parties who are called upon to be witnesses. Helpful information is provided for these parties, who may be confused as to why they are being requested to provide information.

The annulment process combines the difficult task of upholding Our Lord's strong teaching on marriage, yet extending his mercy to those people whose former marriages might have been sacramentally null. *100 Answers to Your Questions on Annulments* should prove to be a highly valuable resource for those interested in this delicate area.

—The Most Reverend John J. Myers, J.D., J.C.D.
Bishop of Peoria, Illinois

Introduction

Each year over 100,000 people, including thousands of non-Catholics, are directly involved in the Church's annulment process. Several times that number of family and friends are immediately affected by the decisions reached in annulment cases. All of these people, to say nothing of observers from the Catholic and the non-Catholic world, have questions about annulments.

Most of the questions contained in these pages are derived from issues which have been posed to me as a canon lawyer, tribunal official, and teacher over the years. Indeed, I have found that people's questions touched on almost every significant aspect of the annulment process, and so it was not difficult to cover most of the key annulment issues in a question-and-answer format. I have tried to answer these questions as I would if they had been posed by someone sitting in my office, that is, simply and accurately.

There are, though, two advantages to answering annulment questions in writing: first, I can add a few extra details to written answers, usually concerning things which people are likely to pose as follow-ups to their original question; second, I can give references to the canon numbers upon which my answers are based. Obviously, I think the answers in this book are correct, but if one wishes to disagree with them, at least it will be clear why I said what I said. Speaking of being clear, I have avoided technical terms as much as possible in these pages, but this is a technical field and precision comes with technical terminology. Major terms are defined in the Glossary.

This book could be read front-to-back, since the questions generally proceed in the same order in which they arise during a typical annulment case. By using the Index, on the other hand, this book could be consulted on a topical basis since there is no need to explain earlier issues if only the later ones are causing confusion. Don't take this book, however, and try to analyze your own marriage, or your parents' marriage, or your children's or your friends' marriage (cf. Question 100). Don't take it to a pastor or tribunal judge and say "See? It says right here this annulment must be granted/denied." Because this book doesn't say that.

Every annulment case is heard under the same set of laws, but no two annulment cases present anything like the same set of facts. The information in this book is provided in the context of a specific question, but even these questions exist in a larger and more complex context. That's why judging is both a science and an art.

It should, in any event, be obvious that this book is designed neither to encourage more annulment cases, nor to discourage them. Actually, this book couldn't do either, since the canon law under which annulment cases are adjudicated is already in force, and the facts which are assessed in an annulment case are already in place before a canon lawyer ever sees them. My hope is to help the people involved in or affected by the annulment process to understand that process better and, where appropriate, to participate in it more effectively. If this, in turn, helps to make sure that the decisions reached by diocesan tribunals in annulment cases are as accurate as possible, I shall be satisfied.

Dr. Edward Neal Peters
7 January 1996

Notes

"1983 CIC" means "1983 Code of Canon Law" (*Codex Iuris Canonici*), promulgated by Pope John Paul II in 1983 and still in force. The number(s) immediately following "1983 CIC" refer to the actual canons of the 1983 Code. All canonical references in this work are to the 1983 Code of Canon Law unless expressly stated otherwise.

"1917 CIC" means "1917 Code of Canon Law" (*Codex Iuris Canonici*), promulgated by Pope Benedict XV in 1917 and no longer in force. The number(s) immediately following "1917 CIC" refer to the actual canons of the 1917 Code.

Unless otherwise noted, diocesan and archdiocesan institutions follow the same rules in marriage cases.

For purposes of readability, some questions and answers are phrased as coming from a husband or a wife, but in no case does the answer depend on the sex of the questioner.

All opinions expressed in this work are the author's. If any opinions expressed herein are not consistent with the mind of the Church, the Church's judgment prevails.

I. Basic Questions on Annulments

Question 1:

What is an annulment?

This might come as a surprise, considering that American tribunals declare well over 50,000 annulments each year, (worldwide some 80,000 annulments are granted by Catholic tribunals annually), but the term "annulment" is nowhere defined in the Code of Canon Law, and in fact, it isn't even used. Nevertheless, it's fairly easy to set out.

An annulment, more accurately termed a declaration of matrimonial nullity, is an official determination by an ecclesiastical tribunal that what appeared to be, from one or more points of view, a valid marriage, was actually not one. An annulment is not a finding that the spouses never really loved each other, nor that the divorce was more one party's fault than the other's, nor that one party is a better Catholic than the other, etc. It is merely (if that word may be used) a juridic determination that, at the time of the wedding,

1

one or both parties to the marriage lacked sufficient capacity for marriage, and/or that one or both parties failed to give adequately their consent to marriage as the Church understands and proclaims it, and/or, in weddings involving at least one Catholic, that the parties violated the Church's requirements of canonical form in getting married.

In finding a marriage null, the Church does not cast blame on either or both parties, even if one or both of them acted in a blameworthy manner. Instead, the Church only states that it does not consider itself, or its members, bound to accept the consequences of the wedding ceremony in question. In practical terms, after nullity is declared, if it's declared, the Church considers the parties of the former, and proven null, marriage free of the marriage bond which would have otherwise arisen therefrom, and hence they are generally free to contract marriage in the Church.

Question 2:

How is an annulment different from a divorce?

I know, of course, that many people refer to annulments as "Catholic divorces," but divorces and annulments differ in a fundamental ways. Still, it might be easier to begin by seeing what they have in common.

A divorce and an annulment are similar in that they both are legal declarations which are necessary before one person can marry another, if either of them had been married before, and the former spouse(s) were not deceased. But that's about where the similarities end and the important differences begin.

A divorce is a civil judicial act whereby what was a civilly valid marriage is officially broken, terminated, ended, finished, *kaput*, whatever word you want to use. The point is, the state makes no secret about its claimed power to separate what it once joined. (I hedge a bit on conceding the state power to separate what it joined because, in many cases, what it joined is a valid marriage under natural law, and hence something the state is not free to tinker with. But that's a different problem.)

An annulment, on the other hand, is an ecclesiastical judicial act whereby what was believed to be a valid marriage is declared never to have been so in the first place. An annulment does not deny that a relationship, perhaps a long and serious one, existed between the parties. It does not imply that parties were "living in sin" or that the children are illegitimate. It only states that, as a matter of objective canon law, what was believed to have been a valid marriage in the eyes of the Church is not so.

There are, by the way, such things as civil annulments which are based on some of the same concepts as ecclesiastical annulments. For example, if someone currently civilly married attempts to marry another person civilly, we call that bigamy. If the second spouse finds out about the prior marriage, he or she can probably sue not so much for a civil divorce, but for a civil annulment of the marriage, based on the prior current marriage of the other party. In such cases, the state generally considers the second spouse not to be divorced, but rather never to have been married at all. Civil annulments, in the relatively rare cases in which they are granted, are not the equivalent of ecclesiastical annulments, even though the concept is similar. Marriages which end in civil annulment must still be adjudicated ecclesiastically before canonical nullity could be declared.

Question 3:

One more time. What's the difference between a divorce and an annulment? They still seem mighty similar to me.

Well, let's try this one: consider automobiles and ambulances. They are both four-wheeled, gasoline-powered vehicles that drive on roads and take people places. They would seem to be rather similar in many respects. Now, let me ask you: this afternoon, would you rather leave work in your car, or in an ambulance? What seems similar in some respects can be as different as night and day in others.

Divorce destroys something that was, annulments recognize that something never was. That is not just semantics, anymore than describing one's trip home from the office as being in a car rather than in an ambulance is just semantics. It's a matter of precision, and hence a matter of truth.

Last night my boys played catch with an apple, but neither of them tried to eat a baseball for supper. There are similarities between divorce and annulments, of course, although these similarities are routinely exaggerated, and even exploited, by the secular media and others. Thoughtful people, however, will avoid treating things like divorces and annulments, which are similar in some respects, as if they were necessarily similar in others.

Question 4:

Whom should I see first about getting an annulment?

Virtually every nullity petition begins with an interview in a pastor's office at the parish level. This is a practically useful, but technically unofficial, part of most diocesan tribunals' procedures. Most pastors (or their staffs) are very willing to assist potential petitioners in drafting their forms for the tribunal. If, however, you have doubts about where to go first, or if you have certain reasons for not wishing to approach your local parish first, you can call or write directly to the diocesan offices for guidance. They are listed in the phone book. Ask for the Tribunal.

You should realize, by the way, that contacting the pastor, or even dropping off your completed nullity petitions with him or the parish staff, is not the official beginning of your petition. Only when the tribunal itself receives and formally accepts your petition do any procedural clocks start ticking. If several weeks, let alone months, have passed since talking with your pastor and you still have not heard anything from the tribunal, check into it. Paperwork can be misplaced or misfiled, or there might be some other problem affecting your petition.

Question 5:

I understand that I need an annulment, but I don't understand why I have to pay for it. It's a Church rule that I have to have an annulment. Why should I have to pay for its rules?

The state required you to get a civil divorce before it would allow you to remarry under its laws, right? Before you got that divorce, the state also required you to pay certain fees and court costs, right? Do you think it was unfair of the state to make you pay for one of its rules?

Technically, of course, you weren't paying for a civil divorce (as if you could literally buy one); instead you were paying for the juridic process by which that divorce was officially effected. Similarly, one does not pay for an annulment (as if they are for sale), rather, one pays for the juridic process by which an annulment might be granted. Notice I say "might" be granted.

Unlike a civil divorce, an annulment is not a more or less automatic, though sometimes traumatic, process in which one has an eventual right to a certain outcome. Because of the Church's commitment to marriage, the annulment process is concerned with very different, and usually much more complex, types of issues than is a civil divorce court. The ecclesiastical process requires the attention of highly trained officials and a qualified supporting staff. Even the documentation and record-keeping required in a marriage case is considerable.

Now, just as a civil court derives its support from a combination of general taxes and specific user fees, so a diocesan tribunal is supported by the general contributions of the faithful and additional fees paid by those using its special services. No one should think, by the way, that diocesan tribunals, American or otherwise, are making money on the annulment process, and indeed, no diocesan tribunal I know of operates in the black. American tribunals generally charge users about one-half of the real cost of a marriage case, and in almost all cases, the out-of-pocket expenses incurred in an ecclesiastical annulment fall far below those incurred in the civil divorce.

Of course, just as with civil courts, where an individual truly cannot meet even their share of the costs, procedures for reducing or waiving tribunal fees are available (1983 CIC 1464 & 1649). No one is ever denied their "day in the tribunal" because of an inability to pay.

Question 6:

How much does an annulment cost?

Costs vary, but typically they will parallel the general cost of living in the United States, tending therefore to be more expensive on the east coast and in urban areas, but less expensive in the midwest and south. Annulment costs fall into three main types.

First and most commonly, there are the basic petition fees payable to the tribunal. This is what most people refer to when they talk about the cost of an annulment. In the U.S., most tribunals charge anywhere from $200 to $1,000 for adjudicating a standard nullity case. A few tribunals charge somewhat over $1,000, and a few charge nothing at all, but *all* tribunals state in advance what their total fee is for processing a petition (1983 CIC 1649). The fee for "documentary cases," however, that is, cases eligible for and heard on the expedited process provided under canon 1686, is usually much less, with $25 or so seeming common. If multiple petitions are presented by the same petitioner at one time, he or she should expect to pay all or most of the standard fee for each case, especially if they are the less expensive documentary cases.

Although there is, strictly speaking, authority on the part of the tribunal to assess fees on both parties in a marriage case (1983 CIC 1649), this is almost never done. Rather, petitioners almost always pay all fees associated with a marriage case. These fees are, however, typically payable over time, if that is more convenient for the petitioner, and there are means for having fees reduced or eliminated in cases of financial hardship (1983 CIC 1464).

In addition to basic tribunal fees, however, there are sometimes additional costs incurred in consulting with medical, psychological, or other experts when that is necessary for resolution of a nullity case (cf. 1983 CIC 1580 & 1649). Again, these fees are usually the responsibility of the petitioner, but in case of doubt, ask.

Finally, some additional costs could be incurred if one were to require, say, certain witnesses to travel a long distance or to produce unusual kinds of evidence (1983 CIC 1571). Or, one might wish to engage a canonical advocate of one's own choosing rather than accepting an advocate supplied by the tribunal. In such cases, it's more likely that the individual requiring such services will be required to pay for them (but see canon 1490, which encourages diocesan tribunals to keep canon lawyers on staff to assist parties in marriage cases). Questions about these potential additional expenses should be presented at the beginning of the case, or in any event as soon as they arise.

What is important to take from all of this is that the stories about $10,000 annulments are myth. Conceivably, if one had filed in the most expensive diocesan tribunal, had used extensive medical and psychological testimony, and had appealed the case through various levels of ecclesiastical courts, one could incur a bill of some thousands of dollars, but such cases are very rare, and most annulments are processed from beginning to end for a small fraction of that.

Question 7:

How long will my annulment take?

Church law requires that tribunals handle all cases as quickly as possible and usually in the order they are received (1983 CIC 1458). From the time your completed application (i.e., all documents submitted and sufficient witnesses responded) is presented to the Tribunal, you should expect a decision in about

12 months (1983 CIC 1453). Cases which present clear canonical grounds for nullity and which are supported by canonically strong evidence can be processed more quickly yet (1983 CIC 1606), but it's important to realize that the tribunal's assessment of these kinds of factors is what counts, not yours.

It is possible to have a nullity case taken out of turn for good reason (1983 CIC 1458), but the tribunal's judgment here is, again, what controls. The "I've-already-booked-a-reception-hall" argument is not usually considered a good reason for a tribunal to take a marriage case out of turn. Reasons which sometimes are accepted as justifying speedier treatment (though not necessarily the desired results) would include the intended entry of a party into the Church at Easter. But, parties—and pastors—should not expect tribunals to drop everything else at the mere sight of an "RCIA case."

The mandatory review which is part of every case in which an annulment is granted can take up to six additional months, but usually it requires less than that. And, for marriage cases which are filed in Rome or which go there on appeal (1983 CIC 1444), there really is no practical time limit. Two to four years is not unusual.

Generally, one should not call the tribunal offices just to ask about the "status" of one's case. These calls only interrupt the heavy work load of the tribunal staff and they cannot speed up your case. Instead, drop them a letter or post-card if you are concerned about the time your case is requiring.

Question 8:

Are annulments easier to get nowadays than they used to be?

Without a doubt, yes. For two very important reasons. First, numerous reforms in the canons which govern matrimonial nullity cases have greatly facilitated the ability of Catholics and non-Catholics to file and pursue marriage nullity petitions in diocesan tribunals. These revisions, placed in Church law by the Holy See (not by creative American canonists) have been in force more or less since the early 1970s, and for the most part have been made standard in the 1983 Code. They included a host of revisions on technical points which, while perhaps escaping the immediate notice of non-canonists, carried an immediate impact on both the number of nullity petitions filed and on the percentage of petitions granted.

Second, reforms in the canons which govern important matters related to matrimonial consent were revised (again, by Rome) in ways that made it much easier to examine directly the matrimonial impact of so many negative, seriously debilitating factors like drug and alcohol abuse, physical and sexual abuse, parental divorce and serial marriage, and other mental and emotional factors. These factors can, and obviously often do, seriously impact marriages before they ever get off the ground, sometimes to the point of canonical nullity. The Congregation for the Doctrine of the Faith, which few could accuse of being lax on marriage, has recognized in its letter on Reception of Communion by Divorced and Remarried Catholics (14 September 1994, Para. 9) the effects of canonical revisions in increasing the chances of proving the canonical nullity of an invalid marriage. In brief, the bases for matrimonial nullity in real life are now easier to identify in canon law.

Understandably, though, the speed and force with which these revisions have impacted Catholic nullity cases, particularly during times in which so much deterioration in other aspects of Catholic life seems to have set in, have caused many to worry, or conclude, that the tribunal process is partly responsible for the on-going collapse in Catholic and American marriage. These criticisms can, and I think should, be rejected without running to the opposite extreme and claiming that diocesan tribunals are flawless in their handling of nullity cases. They aren't; they can't be.

If an analogy may be used here, the revised canons on matrimonial capacity and consent might not serve as a cure for the divorce disease, but they do greatly aid in the diagnosis of the condition. Church teaching on the permanence of marriage has not changed and it never will change. But the Church's ability to determine more precisely just what a null marriage looks like has improved. Admittedly, the sight might not be a pretty one, but it's a more accurate picture than before.

If correctly followed, the annulment process can declare certain people free to marry in the Church who, in justice, ought to be so considered, and it frequently can show them how their earlier attempt(s) at marriage were invalid, making them, one would hope, much less likely to repeat—or be victimized by—the same mistakes again. On the other hand, the annulment process can also affirm for certain people that, notwithstanding their civil divorce and the suffering which precedes and follows it, the Church still considers them married and, in the Truth which sets us free (John 8:32), it expects them to conduct themselves, to the extent they are able, in accord with that status.

Question 9:

Will the length of time two people were married make any difference in an annulment case?

Yes and no. Strictly speaking, the duration of marriage is not proof of either its validity or invalidity, but it could be used as evidence of either. Remember, an annulment case focuses on what happened prior to, and at the time of, the wedding. Any factor which involves post-wedding evidence, such as the length of the marriage, is useful only to the degree that it helps illuminate the parties' status and actions in actually getting married.

For example, a couple who remains together for a long period of time pretty obviously had at least some relational skills and some capacity for life together. That evidence tends to point toward the validity of their marriage. At the same time, canon law recognizes a principal from the middle ages: "What was infirm at the beginning cannot be made firm just by the passage of time." Examples of marriages which lasted many decades, but which still were later proven to be null, can be found.

On the other hand, a couple who remains together for just a few days or weeks, gives some evidence that they really had no idea what marriage was all about in the first place, and therefore it can be argued that they never entered what the Church would recognize as a valid marriage. However, the mere brevity of the marriage, that is, the couple's failure to live in accord with the permanence of marriage, does not necessarily mean that they were incapable of entering a true marriage. Just as above, examples of marriages which "lasted" only a few months, but which could not be proven canonically null, do exist.

Question 10:

Is it true that one cannot receive an annulment if the marriage produced children?

It is not true. The presence of children is not proof that a marriage was valid, and the absence of children is not proof that it was invalid. In fact, neither situation is even evidence of either status.

II. Officials in the Process

Question 11:

Do I have any choice over the judge(s) who will hear my marriage case?

Not really. Judges are appointed to office by the diocesan bishop (1983 CIC 1421), and they are assigned to specific cases by the judicial vicar (1983 CIC 1425 § 3) usually in the order the cases are presented (1983 CIC 1458). That said, if you have reason to object to a certain judge participating in your case, you have the right to make that objection known under canon 1448. The same thing applies to objections against Promoters of Justice and Defenders of the Bond, and even to auditors (1983 CIC 1428 § 1) and probably assessors (1983 CIC 1424) if they are involved in your case. Your objection need not be accepted by the tribunal, although in my experience most tribunals try to accommodate reasonable objections to officers from either petitioners or respondents.

Question 12:

I was quite surprised when I showed up for an interview on my annulment case; I was interviewed by a nun who called herself a judge. I thought all canon lawyers were priests. Is this going to cause a problem in my case?

I have, from time to time, seen the same quick look of surprise in someone's eye when they arrive for a tribunal interview with me, a married layman.

The great majority of canon lawyers are priests, but deacons, religious, and laity are making up a growing percentage of the profession. Canon law requires all tribunal judges to be degreed in canon law (1983 CIC 1421 § 3), but it allows bishops to appoint academically qualified non-clerics as judges in diocesan tribunals (1983 CIC 1421 § 2). Where non-clerics, like myself, serve as judges in tribunals, they do so together with two other clerics, usually priests, serving as collegiate judges.

It can happen, moreover, that one of those three judges, perchance the lay judge, is more active in the instruction of a particular case than are the other two judges for various reasons. For example, the judicial vicar (or his adjutant) might have assigned the lay judge to serve as "ponens," or primary author, of the decision (1983 CIC 1429 & 1610 § 2) which might result from the case. Even though all judges in a collegiate tribunal must pass on the entire acts of a case and decide each case by majority vote (1983 CIC 1426 § 1), one would expect to see the ponens more directly involved in the actual development of the case which he or she might have to write up.

Question 13:

Can bishops grant annulments?

S trictly speaking, yes, but it would be very rare. Canon 1419 § 1 recognizes the diocesan bishop (but not auxiliary, coadjutor, or retired bishops) as the first judge in a diocese, and canon 1425 § 4 could be invoked to allow the diocesan bishop to sit as the sole judge on a marriage case. But all American diocesan bishops have appointed judicial vicars and other judges (1983 CIC 1420–1421) in their dioceses and no bishop that I know of has ever exercised his option to reserve the hearing of marriage cases to himself. If he were to do so, however, he would still be required to follow the canons governing the judgment of marriage cases.

Question 14:

Can pastors grant annulments?

I n so far as they are acting in their capacity as pastors, certainly not. Pastors, as pastors, have no judicial authority under the 1983 Code. But be careful here: under the 1917 Code, which was less strict about judges having canon law degrees than is the 1983 Code, many pastors also served as tribunal judges, at least for certain types of "simpler" cases (e.g., lack of form cases). Some of these synodal and pro-synodal judges, as they were technically known (1917 CIC 1574), served in judicial office until 1993 or so. Conceivably, a few are even yet in judicial office, although in all the cases I have seen, Vatican officials have refused to allow such non-degreed judges to renew their terms of service.

Additional confusion on this point can arise in that many pastors are currently delegated by their bishops to grant certain types of dispensations which are needed in particular marriage situations. Some people might mistakenly think of these dispensations as annulments. In general, if a pastor, or any other priest, claims the authority to annul any type of marriage without going through the diocesan tribunal, check it out.

Question 15:

I have been told that the Defender of the Bond is opposed to my annulment. Who is this Defender of the Bond and what has this got to do with my case?

In 1741, Pope Benedict XIV enacted a major series of canonical reforms, including reforms on the conduct of matrimonial cases in diocesan tribunals. Ever since then, the Defender of the Bond is a tribunal official in every diocese whose task it is to propose, without regard to the opinions of the parties, everything which can be reasonably argued against granting a nullity petition. The role of the Defender, as Pope Pius XII said in 1944, and as Pope John Paul II reaffirmed in the 1983 Code (cf. 1983 CIC 1432), is not to stall marriage cases with a myriad of technicalities, but rather to make sure that all of the evidence in favor of the marriage is carefully considered by the judge(s).

The Defender of the Bond is appointed by the diocesan bishop, and can be either a cleric or a lay person and must be academically degreed in canon law (1983 CIC 1435). The Defender does not work for the respondent nor even, strictly speaking, against the petitioner. The Defender literally defends the bond of marriage which Church law presumes to have arisen from a presumptively valid marriage.

In many of the cases coming before diocesan tribunals (unfortunately for what this says about the state of modern matrimony), there are few reasonable arguments which could be raised against granting a nullity petition, and to such cases the Defender cannot raise substantive objections, although he or she still monitors to make sure that procedural requirements are honored.

But, when a Defender does raise substantive (or procedural, for that matter) objections to declaring nullity in a case, they must be seriously considered by the judge(s). Defenders are usually as well-trained in canon law as judges are. Some Defenders have prior experience as judges, and many judges once served as Defenders. In brief, Defenders and judges usually understand where each other is coming from.

If a Defender of the Bond doesn't like the result in a case, he or she can appeal it to a higher court, even over the objections of both parties to the marriage (1983 CIC 1628). That alone makes Defenders a force to be reckoned with. For all that, though, Defenders do not have veto power over judge(s)' decisions, and their objections to the granting of an annulment can be overruled.

Don't think of the Defender of the Bond as an obstacle to your nullity petition. Think of him or her as a sign of the Church's commitment to canonical quality control in general and to the protection of marriage in particular. If the Defender has objections to your petition, they will be taken seriously. But you still have the right to disagree with the Defender (cf., for example, 1983 CIC 1601–1603) if you feel that the tribunal was wrong in siding with the Defender in denying your petition, and you have the same right to appeal that decision as the Defender had the right to appeal the opposite result.

Question 16:

Who is the Promoter of Justice?

The Promoter of Justice is an official appointed in every diocese by the bishop whose task it is to look after the public good (1983 CIC 1430 & 1435). Like Defenders of the Bond, the Promoter can be either a cleric or a lay person, as long as he or she is degreed in canon law (1983 CIC 1435). Nullity cases do not automatically require the participation of a Promoter, like they do Defenders, but Promoters are allowed to intervene in marriage cases if they feel the public good is at risk (1983 CIC 1430 & 1691). This is unusual, however, and normally the Promoter does not become involved in nullity petitions. About the only time one might see a Promoter becoming involved in a nullity case would be if canon 1674 were being invoked to allow the Promoter to impugn a certain marriage.

Question 17:

May the parties in an annulment case use lawyers?

If by lawyer you mean a civil lawyer (perhaps the one who handled your divorce?) the answer is no. Canon 1481 allows the parties in marriage cases to use canon lawyers, known as advocates, but to qualify as a canonical advocate, one must meet the requirements listed in canon 1483, namely, being at least 18 years old, enjoying a good reputation, being expert in canon law, and being approved by the diocesan bishop. Very few civil lawyers, even divorce lawyers, know anything about canon law, and therefore they would not be qualified to serve as canonical advocates.

There is no requirement, by the way, that either or both parties in a marriage case use canonical advocates, and many nullity cases are conducted without them. This stems from the fact that, while Ameri-

can common law is, appropriately enough, an adver-
sarial system in which lawyers and their clients win
or lose, canon law tends to preserve the Roman
inquiry-based approach in which advocates assist tribunals in the discovery of truth. Theoretically, at least,
no one loses in a marriage case, although that truth
might at times require an exceptionally open mind for
appreciation. When advocates are used, however,
they assume certain rights and responsibilities in the
process which are explained to the parties at the time.

To the surprise of some, there is no requirement
in canon 1483 that advocates be academically degreed
in canon law. Personally, I think the day is coming
when all advocates will have to be degreed in canon
law, but the current law recognizes, correctly, that
some people can have developed very impressive
canonical knowledge and skills, at least in marriage
cases, as a result of long experience in the field.

Many American dioceses use parish priests and
deacons as advocates in marriage cases. Typically, the
priest or deacon who helps the petitioner apply for
the annulment also serves as advocate for that party,
and advocates for respondents are often appointed
from among tribunal staff. Some parishes even have
lay or religious "annulment coordinators" who assist
the parties in their cases, and a few dioceses are
moving toward certification of non-degreed parish
advocates, whether laity or clergy, to help with the
huge marriage case load currently being addressed by
diocesan tribunals.

Nevertheless, and despite my respect for the work
of many non-degreed advocates, the parties to a
marriage case have certain rights in the selection of
the canonical counsel including the right to qualified
counsel. Canon law judges are allowed to be more

flexible in assisting parties to formulate their canonical cases than civil judges are allowed to be (1983 CIC 1452 § 2), but I have still seen nullity cases whose outcome could have been influenced by the quality of the advocate working (or not working, as the case might be) on them.

Question 18:

Can I pick my own canon lawyer?

Generally, yes, but there are a few strings attached. Canon 1481 establishes the right of the parties in all tribunal cases to pick their own canon lawyers, but that same canon also allows parties to act without a canon lawyer under most circumstances if they so choose, and specifically states that automatic counsel need not be appointed by the diocesan tribunal in marriage cases.

On the other hand, diocesan tribunals are encouraged, but not strictly required, to have canon lawyers attached to and paid by the tribunal, being thereby available to assist parties wishing to use them especially in marriage cases (1983 CIC 1490). Most American tribunals probably can say that they meet this exhortation, but often by means of making available persons who are otherwise judges in marriage cases for service as advocates in cases wherein they will not be called upon to render a decision. While such a system is probably not what the Code had in mind, it is, in most cases, I think, a practical way of satisfying

the legitimate, and rising, demand for canonical advo-
cacy services without incurring the large overhead of
retaining designated advocates.

In any event, even if the diocesan tribunal which
is hearing your marriage case has advocates available,
you retain the right to name your own canon lawyer,
provided that he or she meets the standards set forth
in canon 1483, namely, being over 18, possessing a
decent reputation, being expert (though not necessarily degreed) in canon law, and being approved by the
local bishop. This last clause—being approved by the
local bishop—is meant to be taken seriously, of
course, but so is one's basic right to name one's own
canonical advocate. The trend seems to be toward
allowing parties as much freedom as possible in naming their own advocates, if not because such a policy
is more consistent with canon law, then because those
usually requested to serve as personal advocates are
almost always academically degreed and well-trained,
and because the fees incurred thereby are usually the
responsibility of the party choosing them. Conceivably, however, a party wishing to name an advocate,
especially one from outside the diocese, might be told
that a given tribunal does not accept outside advocates. Such an answer is, I think, canonically illegal,
and there are means available to you and your intended advocate to contest that decision.

A few additional points. One can name several
advocates to serve simultaneously (1983 CIC 1482 § 3)
although this would rarely be needed, and written
appointments of advocates, known as "mandates,"
must be presented to the tribunal at the beginning of
representation (1983 CIC 1484 § 1). Once appointed,
advocates assume certain rights and duties (cf. generally canons 1482–1489) which are explained at the

time of appointment, but it is useful to know that one can remove one's own advocate at any time by giving notice to the advocate and to the judge (1983 CIC 1486 § 1). Moreover, for serious cause, an advocate can be removed from office by the judge (1983 CIC 1487).

Question 19:

What role would the priest who married us play in our annulment case?

He need not play any role. There is no canonical requirement that the official witness to a wedding (1983 CIC 1108 & 1112) be made part of an annulment case on that wedding. On the other hand, either or both parties could ask that the officiating minister be called as a witness in the case. Normally, one would only do that if the minister had significant knowledge of either or both parties independently of the ceremony, but if, say, some serious situation affecting the ceremony itself was in question, it would make sense to bring in the minister to testify about it.

III. Where Can Annulment Cases Be Heard?

Question 20:

Where can my annulment petition be heard?

I assume you know that virtually all marriage cases are heard in diocesan tribunals, the offices of which are usually located in or very near diocesan administrative centers (look for them in the phone book), and that what you really want to know is which tribunal or tribunals would be "competent," or canonically qualified, to hear your case. The rules on tribunal competence, that is, the authority of a given diocesan tribunal to adjudicate a marriage case, are generous, but they must be followed carefully lest the results of a case be subject to nullification (1983 CIC 1620). The tribunal will, of course, handle issues related to competence, but an explanation of what they are doing might be helpful.

Canon 1673 determines which diocesan tribunals can hear a case, and is divided into four subsections, any one of which is sufficient to establish canonical competence to hear a case.

A) Place of wedding. The tribunal of the diocese where the wedding was celebrated, known canonically as "the forum of contract," is always competent to hear a nullity petition on that marriage. This rule applies even if one or both spouses have since left that diocese, and even if they were only there long enough for the wedding to take place and they never had any intention of remaining there. It also applies regardless of the possible objection of the respondent, whose opinion on this point need not even be solicited. And it applies to cases of non-Catholic weddings, even if neither party has since become Catholic. Note: if the wedding to be impugned was a Catholic wedding, but one which had been preceded by a civil wedding, it is the place of the Catholic wedding, not the civil ceremony, which is considered the forum of contract.

B) Place of the respondent. The tribunal of the diocese where the respondent has canonical domicile or quasi-domicile, known canonically as "the forum of the respondent," is always competent to hear a nullity petition on that marriage. While there are a few technical variations on this rule (such as in cases dealing with transient or mentally incompetent respondents), basically, this rule means that any diocese wherein the respondent is living, and has lived for at least three months (sometimes less), is competent to hear a petition on that respondent's marriage (cf. generally canons 100–107). This rule applies even if the petitioner has never been to the respondent's forum and applies even if neither party is Catholic. As was true for forum of contract, the rules on forum of the respondent apply regardless of the possible objection of the respondent, whose opinion on this point need not even be solicited. Moreover, even if the respondent leaves the territory after the tribunal has obtained jurisdiction over the case (1983 CIC 1512, n.2), the petition can still be heard.

C) Place of the petitioner. Under certain circumstances, the petitioner can submit his or her marriage case to the tribunal where he or she currently lives, regardless of where the wedding took place or where the respondent currently lives. This is often more convenient for the petitioner, and thousands of marriage cases are heard this way each year. But the rules are a little trickier.

First, the petitioner must canonically have a domicile, not just a quasi-domicile, in the diocese in which he or she wishes to file the nullity petition. This means that the petitioner must have, at some point, moved into the diocese with the intention of remaining there unless called away (1983 CIC 102). Note that domicile for the petitioner (or respondent, for that matter) can be acquired immediately. This might sound a little strange at first, and it could strike some as a vague rule, but in practice it's fairly easy to assess accurately. Moreover, regardless of one's intention about staying in a diocese, mere residence in the diocese for five years automatically confers domicile.

Second, both parties must live in the territory of the same conference of bishops. In most cases, this simply means that both parties must live in the same country, since most episcopal conferences cover one and only one nation (1983 CIC 448 § 1). In the United States, though, there are some American territories which do not belong to the National Conference of

Catholic Bishops: for example, Puerto Rico, Guam and other U.S. possessions in the South Pacific are not considered part of the U.S. for purposes of matrimonial jurisdiction under canon 1673, n.3. On the other hand, the Virgin Islands are part of the U.S. for purposes of canon 1673, n.3.

Third, it's up to the judicial vicar of the diocese where the respondent has domicile to consent to the request for competence from the petitioner's diocese. Without that consent, the case cannot be heard in the petitioner's home diocese. Before granting such consent, the judicial vicar of the respondent must hear, or get the opinion of, the respondent to the request from petitioner's home diocese. Note that it's not required that the respondent agree to the request, only that his or her judicial vicar have gotten the views of the respondent (even a non-Catholic respondent) on the matter.

Most requests for competence made under canon 1673, n.3, are granted, probably because most respondents do not in fact oppose a "foreign" tribunal hearing their case. The few respondents who do express objections, usually object to any tribunal hearing the case, something which respondents clearly have no right to insist upon.

If, on the other hand, a respondent expresses objections based on, say, serious inconvenience in participation, they have a better chance of getting their judicial vicar to withhold the desired consent. It is not necessary for respondents to use technical words in expressing their objections, as long as they are clear enough in their objections to give their judicial vicar a reason to say no. Of course, if the respondent's judicial vicar does say no, there is nothing to prevent the petitioner from then filing his or her case in the respondent's diocesan tribunal on the basis of canon 1673, n.2, (residence of the respondent) or in the place of contract under canon 1673, n.1, if that is different.

D) Place of proofs. Under certain circumstances, a petitioner can seek to have his or her petition filed in any convenient tribunal, provided that the selected tribunal can be shown to be what canon law considers the "forum of proofs" under canon 1673, n.4. In some respects this is similar to the "forum of petitioner" discussed above.

In these kinds of cases, the petitioner approaches a diocesan tribunal (not necessarily one in which the petitioner has domicile or quasi-domicile) and asks them to consider accepting the case under canon 1673, n.4, the "forum of proofs." The petitioner provides evidence that the tribunal really is the forum wherein the evidence in the case could be best collected as might be the case, for example, if several of the witnesses who knew the details of the marriage were located in or near that diocese, and/or if important documents are more easily produced there than in other places.

The diocesan tribunal would still have to obtain the consent of the judicial vicar of wherever the ex-spouse has domicile, but unlike the situation under canon 1673, n.3, there is no requirement under canon 1673, n.4, that the respondent live in the territory of the same episcopal conference as the petitioner. That difference makes canon 1673, n.4, a basis for jurisdiction in some of the more unusual cases, for example, cases involving parties from different countries.

Finally, one should note that there is no preference among the four bases for jurisdiction listed above, and they can be pursued at the petitioner's choice (1983 CIC 1407 § 3 & 1415). In other words, there is no requirement that petitioners file in the forum of contract before filing in the forum of respondent, etc.

Question 21:

My former wife and I were married in a third world country. After our divorce, I came to America and I was planning to seek an annulment. However, I have been told that I will have to have my case heard in that country because my ex-wife still lives there. Is this true?

Not necessarily. There are two possible ways to have your case heard in the United States (or any other nation, for that matter).

First, you can present your petition to any convenient U.S. tribunal and ask them to consider accepting the case under canon 1673, n.4, the "forum of proofs." (They would probably have hit on that idea themselves, but your suggesting it could save time.) You would need to provide evidence that the U.S. tribunal really is the forum wherein the proofs are best collected as might be the case, for example, if several of the witnesses who knew the details of the marriage had also moved to the U.S. with you.

The American tribunal would still need the consent of the judicial vicar of wherever your ex-spouse has canonical domicile, and neither you nor the tribunal can force that consent. I have seen many such requests granted, however, on the basis that third-world tribunals do not enjoy making petitioners wait three, four, or five years for a decision, which often is the situation in marriage cases. Unlike canon 1673, n.3, there is no requirement under canon 1673, n.4, that your former spouse live in the territory of the same episcopal conference that you do. Confusion on this point might have led whomever you consulted to say that your nullity petition had to be heard in the country wherein your ex-wife still lives.

If the forum-of-proofs approach fails, you could consider approaching the Supreme Tribunal of the Apostolic Signatura in the Vatican for "prorogation" of competence to a tribunal more convenient to you. Such permissions are not commonly granted, especially where the foreign tribunal was willing to accept the case, but neither are they unheard of. Seek canonical advice before attempting to contact the Signatura.

You could, of course, file your case in your home country. It may be slower (but see canon 1453, suggesting one year as the basic time limit on deciding cases), but at least you are in the system, somewhere.

Question 22:

Can I file my nullity petition in Rome?

Yes, (cf. 1983 CIC 1417 § 1 & 1444), but why would you want to? It is almost certainly going to be slower, more expensive, and generally more cumber-

some than proceeding in a local tribunal. Besides, if
you are not satisfied with the results of the local
tribunal process, you still have the right of appeal to
Rome (1983 CIC 1628).

Question 23:

If I move away after filing my nullity petition, will the tribunal still hear the case?

P robably, especially if the tribunal has formally
accepted the case and cited the respondent since
it has probably acquired jurisdiction over the case
thereby (1983 CIC 1512, n.2). On the other hand, if
you anticipate moving rather soon after filing your
nullity case, you might tell the tribunal about that
because your absence could make the investigation of
the case more difficult. It could even be to your
advantage to hold off filing your petition until you
reach your new diocese. If you do move, though,
there are means for trying to have your case trans-
ferred to a more convenient, but still competent,
diocesan tribunal, generally by "renouncing" your first
filing under canon 1524.

Question 24:

Will I have to appear for an interview if I file a nullity petition?

As the petitioner, you should certainly be prepared and willing to appear, but you will not necessarily be called (1983 CIC 1530 & 1528). Although tribunals vary in their approaches here, many tribunals tend to schedule interviews only if there are serious questions potentially affecting the outcome of the case which require resolution prior to sentence.

It sometimes happens, of course, that petitioner and respondent declarations are so clear and detailed in themselves, and enjoy credible support from witness, that the tribunal can reach a decision (whether affirmative or negative) based on them without additional interviews (cf. also 1983 CIC 1606, expressly allowing for a speedy decision in such cases). Likewise, the instruction of the case might reveal a failure to observe canonical form or an undispensed impediment, obviating the need for a formal trial at all (1983 CIC 1686).

Often, however, conflicts or discrepancies exist in testimony, or significant gaps in the narration exist. In such cases the tribunal is more likely to call for an interview with either or both parties. Sometimes witnesses, too, are ask to supplement their testimony, either in writing or by means of an interview.

Question 25:

Since filing my petition for nullity, I guess you could say I've had second thoughts. Can I cancel the case?

Assuming the case has not already been decided, you as the petitioner probably can stop the proceedings.

First, under canon 1524, you could notify the tribunal in writing of your desire to "renounce the instance." Your request for renunciation of the case is then communicated to the respondent who is allowed a brief (but canonically unspecified) period in which to accept, or at least not to oppose, your request. If this period passes uneventfully, the judge is then authorized (and probably required, but the Code of Canon Law is not clear on this point) to accept the renunciation. If the respondent objects to your request, the judge again is probably authorized to decide whatever he, or they, think is best. In my experience, virtually all requests for renunciation are granted. Tribunals have more than enough to do deciding cases in which people want answers without deciding cases in which people don't want answers.

(Note: For the occasional respondent who still wishes the case to go forward despite petitioner's renunciation, my advice would be to state your objections to the renunciation but, when renunciation is granted, as it probably will be, to then turn around and become the petitioner in a new filing. Your former spouse cannot stop you from filing your own petition in accord with canon law, even if he or she withdrew theirs.)

Generally, petitioners who renounce the instance are free to reopen their petition upon request at a later time. This happens, for example, in cases where renunciation was requested and granted because witnesses failed to come forward on the case, but with the passage of time (and the healing of feelings?) they have decided to cooperate. It is the right of the tribunal, however, in such cases, to seek updating of already submitted depositions and testimony, lest petitioners simply submit time-sensitive materials when it suits them, regardless of their usefulness to the tribunal.

The second way to stop a case, but a rather riskier one, I think, is simply to fail to respond to the tribunal's communications for six months (1983 CIC 1520). This is called "abatement" and is meant to give tribunals a way out of deciding cases in which the parties seem to have lost interest in the outcome even if they do not actually say so. But, as is always true whenever intentions are gleaned from lack of action, confusion can arise with "abatement." This is especially true for respondents, since their failure to respond to tribunal inquiries could be taken as contumacy and their silence, as it were, held against them (1983 CIC 1531 § 2 & 1592–1595). Moreover, the mere fact that one has not heard from the tribunal for over six months does not necessarily mean that the case is abated. That could simply be tribunal backlog at work.

If a petitioner really wishes to stop a case from going forward, the canons on renunciation should be followed.

IV. When an Annulment Might Be Needed

Question 26:

I already have a civil divorce, but I have been told that I also need an annulment before getting married in Church again. Is that so?

You have been advised correctly. A civil divorce (or for that matter, a civil annulment) does nothing to affect one's marital status in the Church. Canon 1401, n.1, states that the Church alone adjudicates cases dealing with spiritual matters, such as annulment petitions, and canon 1671 adds that the marriage cases of all the baptized (not just Catholics) can be treated under canon law. In the United States, civil law does not recognize ecclesiastical annulments; the Catholic Church does not recognize civil divorces anywhere.

Question 27:

Please explain one thing for me. Long before I was Catholic, I was married and divorced, and then I remarried and have been blessed with many years of happiness ever since. I am planning to enter the Church, but there is all this concern about my first marriage. I understand that Catholics are not allowed to divorce, and I will not get divorced as a Catholic. But why should that first marriage from my non-Catholic days be of such concern? It was over years ago. I feel as if I'm now being held to rules that didn't apply to me then.

Another, if perhaps blunter, way of putting your question would be to ask whether the Church accepts the validity of non-Catholic marriages. Good Heavens, I hope it does, and in fact the Church does presume the validity of non-Catholic marriages.

At the risk of some over-simplification, anything that more or less looks like a marriage among non-Catholics is going to be presumed by the Church to have been a marriage, and hence worthy of the respect due to marriage. What you are being held to is not so much the Church's law on marriage, but what the Church considers to be God's law on marriage. In most cases, that implies permanence (lasting till death) and exclusivity (having only one spouse) in marriage (reflected in, but not derived from, 1983 CIC 1056). But maybe you still don't see the difference? Try this:

Canonical form, for example, is a creation of ecclesiastical law and it applies only to Catholics. You are not being held to canonical form—meaning, by the way, that you cannot use canonical form issues to impugn your non-Catholic wedding, although the Church generally expects some type of religious or civil wedding ceremony between non-Catholics. On the other hand, basic matrimonial capacity and consent issues, being based at least in part on divine or natural law, could bind even non-Catholics, and hence could be used as the basis for challenging even a non-Catholic marriage.

Thus, whatever kind of first marriage you went through seems to meet the very minimal requirements for a presumably valid, albeit non-Catholic, marriage, and hence, for as long as your former spouse is alive, the Church will consider you bound by that first marriage unless and until its nullity is proven in accord with canon law.

Question 28:

After my divorce, I got married again. That was several years ago. I am now hoping to come into the Church. Will I need an annulment of my first marriage, and if it's granted, will I need to get married again in the Church?

Assuming your first spouse is still alive (and assuming that things like Pauline Privilege do not apply in your case), then yes, you will need to have your first marriage assessed in a formal nullity case, and your petition might, or might not, result in an annulment. As to your need to undergo another marriage upon entering the Church, however, assuming that your first marriage is found null, that is another matter.

Catholics are bound to observe the laws of the Church and in a special way the canons concerning marriage. That law, for all the obvious reasons, prohibits Catholics from entering second marriages while the first spouse is still alive (1983 CIC 1085 § 1). Therefore, Catholics who have gone through any kind of marriage ceremony should not, even after a civil divorce, attempt another marriage until the status of that first marriage has been adjudicated by an ecclesiastical court. This rule applies even where it seems perfectly obvious that the first attempt at marriage was null (1983 CIC 1085 § 2).

There are several reasons for this rule. First, what sure looked like a null marriage might, upon qualified examination, be shown, if not valid (for no marriage can ever be proven valid), at least worthy of the presumption of validity. Only a tribunal—not the parties, not pastors, not spiritual advisors—can make that kind of technical determination. Second, family and friends can be scandalized or just plain confused by privates parties determining for themselves which of their marriages ought be valid and which ones should not, and the action of a qualified institution such as the diocesan tribunal can answer their unspoken questions and alleviate unvoiced concerns. Finally, the Church as a community has an interest in keeping track of who is married to whom, and that cannot be accomplished if its members feel free to enter and leave marriages upon their own initiatives.

If you had been Catholic all along, and your second marriage took place outside the Church (i.e., canonical form was not observed), then, even if your first marriage was later proven to have been null, you will still not be considered married in the eyes of the Church until your second marriage is "convalidated" (1983 CIC 1056) or, as many people call it, "blessed in the Church." In very unusual circumstances, your second marriage could even be "radically sanated" (1983 CIC 1161–1165).

On the other hand, if you (and your second spouse) were not Catholic at the time of your second marriage—and hence not bound by canonical form—then your second marriage is automatically going to be considered valid by the Church effective from the date you entered that second marriage upon proof that the first marriage was invalid. An example might help.

Two baptized non-Catholics marry and divorce. One of them marries again, and later wishes to enter the Church. The fact of having two apparent marriages is an obstacle to full communion, right? So, an annulment petition on the first marriage is filed. Assuming grounds for nullity are identified and canonically proven, then that first marriage is null. That means, though, that at the time the spouse entered the second marriage, Church law considered him or her free to marry. But, not being Catholic, and hence not being bound by canonical form, that person was free to enter marriage when he or she went through the second ceremony. Such a person, then, is already considered married under canon law, and upon reception into the Church, he or she need not convalidate their marriage.

Question 29:

My former husband and I were married in a Catholic ceremony. We divorced several years later, and I did not remarry. About one year ago, he died. I've wondered many times over the years if our marriage was really valid, and just for my own peace of mind, I'd like to know. My pastor, however, has told me that the tribunal will not hear a marriage case after one of the spouses dies. Is that correct?

Your pastor is correct. Canon 1675 § 1 states that a marriage which has not been impugned while both spouses were still alive cannot be impugned after the death of either or both spouses. The only exception to this rule would be if the question of the validity of the marriage were important to the resolution of some other canonical or civil question.

Question 30:

I was married in the Church, and later divorced. I remarried outside of the Church, and have remained married since then. I admit that this marriage is invalid in the Church's eyes. Recently, I learned that my ex-spouse had died. My question is: if I want to get my marriage blessed in the Church, do I still need to have an annulment of my first marriage?

No, because the death of your first spouse releases you from the bond of marriage which, you seem to see correctly, the Church presumes to have arisen from your first marriage. I would only note that the mere death of your former spouse does not "validate," as it were, your second marriage (assuming it took place before the death of your former spouse). You do need to renew your consent to marriage in what canon law calls a "convalidation," but what most people simply refer to as "having a marriage blessed in the Church" (cf. 1983 CIC 1156–1160).

Question 31:

As a result of a very complicated set of facts surrounding an unresolved accident my wife had several years ago, the civil courts declared her dead, even though we never recovered her body. I am getting conflicting opinions on whether I need an annulment before getting married again. Please advise.

I can imagine you are getting differing stories. This is an unusual case.

If you received a certificate of death, then the mere fact that a body was not recovered (as say might happen in a ship sinking or earthquake) does not negate the fact that the certain death of one spouse ended the bond of marriage for the surviving spouse. If on the other hand, the spouse's absence is due to something like a "missing and presumed dead" situation (say, the ship sank, but there are reasonable questions as to whether the spouse was actually on the ship), or if the spouse has simply disappeared for an extended period of time, then the Church is going to consider the "surviving" spouse bound by the marriage unless one of three things happens:

1) the other spouse is actually located, living or deceased, and the matter is handled accordingly; or, 2) the marriage is annulled using the regular laws on annulment, including those on proceeding in case of an absent respondent; or, 3) the diocesan bishop, after a thorough investigation, canonically decrees the presumed death of the missing spouse (1983 CIC 1707).

As mentioned above, the mere absence of the spouse, even for many years, and even if civil law regards him or her as dead, does not allow a bishop to decree that spouse as dead. There has to be some evidence of actual death as well.

If a spouse is decreed as "presumed dead" according to canon 1707, the other spouse is considered canonically free to marry in the Church. But, if the original spouse is still alive, the second marriage is null, even though it was entered into in the best of faith by both parties. If there are, therefore, legitimate grounds to petition the nullity of the marriage, and if sufficient evidence of nullity can be adduced, it is probably more prudent to consider such a process before resorting to a "presumed death" procedure.

Question 32:

My husband and I were married in a Catholic ceremony, and later we divorced, but we did not seek an annulment. We recently reconciled and remarried each other before a justice of the peace. Do we need to have our first marriage annulled, and then be remarried by a priest?

No. Marriages celebrated in the Church are presumed valid until a Church court declares them otherwise (1983 CIC 1060). Your civil divorce did nothing to change things from the Church's point of view. There would seem to me, therefore, no requirement that you either file for an annulment of your "first" marriage, or that you "renew" your vows.

Question 33:

I've been divorced for several years and have no intention of remarrying. In fact, I've been thinking about applying for admission to a religious order. I will certainly tell them about my marriage and divorce, but is there a chance I might have to apply for an annulment even to join religious life?

Yes, there is a very good chance you will (1983 CIC 643 § 1, n.2). The same applies if you are considering entrance into a secular institute (1983 CIC 721 § 1, n.3) or society of apostolic life (1983 CIC 735 § 2) to say nothing of some forms of holy orders (1983 CIC 277 & 1041, n.1). Dispensations which would allow a canonically married (even if civilly divorced) person to enter consecrated life or certain forms of holy orders are sometimes possible, but they are unlikely if the annulment process has not been tried first.

V. Questions on Eligibility to File Annulment Cases

Question 34:

May the spouse who filed for the divorce also file for the annulment?

Yes. For a long time in Church law, the fact of having filed for the civil divorce could have been (not that it always was) considered as evidence of being "responsible" for the break-up of the marriage. Since the early 1970s, however, canonical restrictions which prevented "guilty" spouses from submitting their marriage cases have been dropped. Today, therefore, it makes little difference, canonically or practically, whether the petitioner or the respondent filed for the civil divorce.

Question 35:

Is a civil divorce necessary before filing for an annulment?

Virtually every diocesan tribunal in America requires proof of a civil divorce before accepting a canonical nullity petition. The reason usually given for such a policy is, however, I think, quite unsatisfying: many tribunals apparently fear that they can be sued by irate spouses for "alienation of affection" if they accept a nullity petition before there is a civil divorce between the parties. Now, in this day in which no legal theory is too novel for some civil court somewhere to accept, I cannot say that such a fear is utterly groundless.

But, one can be civilly sued for almost anything at almost any time. So what? Remember that annulments in America have no civil effects and that they are, I would argue, purely exercises in religious rights motivated by theological beliefs. That, in my opinion, would deserve some respect by civil courts, too, for all sorts of weighty constitutional reasons. Don't get me wrong: I don't think Catholic dioceses should go around looking for fights with secular courts. But neither do I think they should be forced to curb their own important ecclesial operations just to suit some civil lawyer's theory of state power over churches.

Do I hold, therefore, that the "divorce before annulment requirement" is a bad idea? No. If nothing else, a civil divorce is a practical way of determining that there is no realistic hope of reconciling the parties, something tribunal judges are required to verify as part of every tribunal case, marriage-related or otherwise (1983 CIC 1676).

The "divorce before annulment requirement" works in the great majority of cases, and if one is planning to remarry, a civil divorce is going to be necessary anyway. But if for unusual reasons a civil divorce cannot be procured, that fact standing alone should not be held sufficient to reject a petitioner's libellus (1983 CIC 1505 § 2). In case of serious disputes over this point with your diocesan tribunal, you should seek independent canonical advice.

Question 36:

I am not planning to marry again, but since my divorce I have sometimes wondered whether I should apply for an annulment. Am I eligible to apply even if I am not planning to remarry?

Your intention, or your lack of intention, to marry again is irrelevant to your right to petition for an annulment. Although many people do not apply for an annulment until they are in, or are considering entering, another marriage. many others do petition for a declaration of nullity just for their own "peace of mind."

Generally, there is some advantage to the petitioner (and respondent) in filing a nullity petition sooner than later. Memories are fresher and usually more accurate. Witnesses are still available, documents are easier to find, and so on. Every tribunal judge has seen marriage cases in which plausible grounds for nullity were put forward fail because the long period which had passed between the time of the marriage and the time of filing the nullity petition made it impossible to prove the petitioner's claims.

There is, sometimes, a second advantage to filing marriage cases sooner than later: namely, the personally beneficial effects experienced by many as a result of going through a process which requires an honest, dispassionate review of a traumatic experience. Every tribunal judge knows of people who said that the divorce did little to close the books on a traumatic marriage and divorce, but that the tribunal process was a great help in that regard.

Question 37:

My divorce was some time ago, and for a long time I had no intention of ever getting married again. Now I've met someone and we're engaged. I'm willing to file for an annulment, but I wonder whether I should say anything about being engaged. Will that not look bad to them?

Since your intentions regarding remarriage are, strictly speaking, irrelevant to your right to file a petition of nullity, there is no reason to hide the fact of your engagement. Indeed, there seems some risk of raising questions about your full frankness with the tribunal if you do hide the fact from them and they find out about it from other sources, which happens often enough. Most tribunals will ask you about potential marriage plans anyway, and actual deception regarding that fact can be held against you—although even then, it's probably not enough to scuttle your nullity petition since marriage cases ultimately turn upon different issues than one's future marriage plans. In reality, most of the petitioners in tribunal cases are either already remarried or are hoping to remarry in the near future. Your hopes or plans to remarry place you, therefore, in a big, and canonically innocuous, boat; any deception by you on this point would place you in a small, and conspicuous, boat.

When diocesan tribunals ask about future marriage plans, it's usually for one of three reasons: first, if there are plans for a future wedding, the tribunal will go out of its way to explain time tables and potential problems which might interfere with those marriage plans, lest you or others be surprised and disappointed if things don't work out (for example, your annulment might not be granted or, if granted, a prohibition against future marriage might be imposed); second, the tribunal might wish to do a preliminary assessment of the eligibility of a prospective spouse to enter marriage in the Church, lest problems with an intended spouse's freedom to marry cause problems even if your own case is approved; third, if the intended spouse had a role in the break-up of the first marriage, the tribunal had better hear about it from you rather than from your ex-spouse or witnesses. Although adultery is no longer an impediment to future marriage like it was under the 1917 Code (cf. 1917 CIC 1075, n.1), it is still an important piece of information for the tribunal to have as it attempts to determine matrimonial capacity and consent at the time of the wedding.

Question 38:

I think my marriage was null, but I can't go in there and claim that I never loved my former wife, because I did love her. I can't say that there weren't any good times together, because there were. I know it, she knows it, and God knows it. Should I even bother to file for annulment?

Whether you file for an annulment is up to you, and whether your petition is accepted and eventually granted would be up to the tribunal system acting in accord with canon law. But having loved your former spouse and having shared good times together is no more a bar to your filing a nullity petition than having failed to love your spouse and never having shared any good times together would be sufficient to grant your petition. While love and happy memories are more likely in healthy marriages, they are not, strictly speaking, the kinds of things that nullity cases are decided upon.

An annulment does not necessarily imply that there was no love between the parties nor that they never shared any good times. Similarly, the failure to get an annulment does not mean that the tribunal decided that the couple loved each other and enjoyed the experience of marriage. As I have said many times, all nullity cases turn upon, and only upon, issues related to capacity, consent, and form. Love and happy experiences, or the lack thereof, might shed some light on the kinds of issues which concern tribunals, but they are not themselves the issues upon which tribunals decide cases.

Question 39:

After my divorce, I fell away from the Church. Actually, I haven't been in a church for over 15 years. If I wanted to have my marriage reviewed for the possibility of an annulment, would my lengthy absence from the Catholic Church be held against me? I'd understand if it did, but I was wondering anyway.

Failure to practice one's Faith is a serious matter, of course, but it would not prevent you from filing a marriage petition, nor would it be grounds for the tribunal to reject your petition. The scenario you describe is not uncommon, and often enough an annulment is part of one's return to the practice of the Faith.

Question 40:

My husband and I have been happily married for over 30 years in the Presbyterian Church. After several years of prayer and study I have decided to become Catholic. My husband does not object but he has no interest in joining the Catholic Church himself. My husband had been married very briefly before he met me. He and his first wife were divorced before he and I ever met. I've been told that this is an obstacle to my entering the Catholic Church, but that if his first marriage were annulled, we would be considered validly married for Catholic purposes, and I would be free to enter the Church. My problem is that my husband has no interest in asking for a Catholic annulment. I've been told that I am not eligible to file a case for him. What can I do, if anything, to clear this up?

Y our question is complicated, but it's not unheard of. It is, I think, going to be encountered more frequently as Catholic evangelism efforts toward Protestant denominations result in the conversion of one, canonically free-to-marry, spouse, while the other spouse has an apparent matrimonial history which, understandably, he or she has no interest in resolving.

The canonical problem, as you have experienced, is that you have no power to impugn the former marriage of your current spouse which is preventing your entry into the Church (1983 CIC 1674). There are, however, a couple of ways of approaching things.

First, you should really try to ask your husband whether he is willing to file a nullity petition in his own name, even if, as you say, he has no interest in the outcome. Perhaps putting him in touch with someone who can explain the situation to him better than you can would help. It might take time, but some people in your husband's position do eventually decide to cooperate if only for the sake of the spouse for whom this process is important. But suppose you have tried that (and I mean really tried that) to no avail.

There is one other way of impugning a marriage, but it requires getting a tribunal official known as the Promoter of Justice involved. The Promoter is the one other person who can impugn a marriage, at least under certain circumstances. The procedure I'm about to describe is very unusual, but it's quite within the law.

Under canon 1674, n.2, the Promoter of Justice can impugn a marriage if the nullity of the marriage has become widely known, and the marriage cannot be convalidated (in effect, repaired) or at least such is not expedient. Before explaining these terms, it's important to realize canon 1674 notably increases the authority of Promoters to impugn marriage over what they used to enjoy under the older 1917 Code.

Under the 1917 Code, the Promoter of Justice could impugn a marriage only if it was invalid due to an impediment, and what is more, not just any impediment would do, but only an impediment which was by its nature canonically public (1917 CIC 1971 § 1, n.2). Thus, under the 1917 Code, the Promoter could impugn a marriage based on, for example, nonage (extreme youth) because insufficient age at the time of the wedding is an impediment, and moreover one which could be proven in the external forum by documents such as birth certificates, etc. But, under the 1917 Code, if the marriage was invalid because of "non-public impediments," or because of a failure to give proper consent, or because canonical form was not correctly followed, there was nothing the Promoter could do about it, and the marriage could be impugned only by one of the two parties two it. The situation such as the one you described above, therefore, could not have been addressed under the 1917 Code.

But the 1983 Code reads very differently on this point. No longer is the Promoter of Justice limited to impugning only marriages which are invalid based on public impediments. Now, any grounds of nullity can be argued by the Promoter, including failures of consent and improper canonical form. Nor is there any requirement that the grounds of nullity proposed by the Promoter be canonically public. Of course, the Promoter must still prove his case against the marriage, but at least now he is authorized to present it to the diocesan tribunal for consideration.

The only current restrictions on the authority of the Promoter of Justice to impugn a marriage are that the nullity of the marriage must be "divulged," and that convalidation of that marriage must be impossible or at least inexpedient. The Code does not define these conditions further, but a good case can be made that marriage which ended in divorce several decades earlier, especially if it was the type of marriage that is more easily proven null, can be said to be widely recognized as null, and that where the parties have gone on to other marriages, often producing children of their own, perhaps having lost all contact with each other, the case can likewise be made that trying to convalidate the earlier marriage is, to put it mildly, inexpedient. The situation you described seems to me to meet several, perhaps all, of these criteria, and it's certainly worth considering if your husband still declines to enter a case in his own name.

Don't be put off if, having suggested a Promoter of Justice case, you are told something like "We don't do those here" or "They are too complicated for our tribunal." Most Promoters have not tried such a case before and they might well be reluctant to attempt one. On the other hand, the law is there to be used, and it has been reformed to make it easier to use. Granted, there are some technical issues beyond the scope of this book which have to ironed out in particular cases, but a good canon lawyer should be able to assist you.

Canon 1752, in a sort of off-hand manner, closes the 1983 Code of Canon Law by stating that canonical equity and the salvation of souls are always the supreme law of the Church. The situation you describe surely merits consideration from both points of view.

Question 41:

I know this might sound strange, but here goes. I'm divorced, but I'm not Catholic. Neither was my ex. I'm not planning to join the Catholic Church, but I am thinking about getting married again (not to a Catholic, by the way). The Protestant denomination I belong to does not have an annulment process like yours. They feel that a civil divorce is sufficient. I don't feel completely comfortable with their position. Would it be possible to have your people take a case like mine, and tell me what they thought about it?

First, you are free to seek informal opinions on your first marriage from anybody you like, and the quality of the opinion(s) you get would depend on the knowledge and good sense of your advisor(s), plus on the accuracy of the information you share. But you seem to be asking something more, namely, whether you can actually submit a nullity petition to a diocesan tribunal, and get a formal decision from them, even if you are not canonically bound by that decision.

The answer to that question is yes, you can submit your petition to a Catholic tribunal (1983 CIC 1476) and receive a formal sentence. The canonical restrictions against non-Catholics approaching diocesan tribunals with cases have been lifted, more or less, since shortly after the Second Vatican Council, and canon law expressly asserts the right of the Church to adjudicate the marriage cases of all the baptized, Catholic or otherwise (1983 CIC 1671, 1055 § 2, & 1400–1401). Admittedly, most of the nullity petitions which diocesan tribunals receive from non-Catholics are prompted by the desire of one (or both) of the parties to enter the Church or to marry a Catholic, but neither condition is a requirement for filing a nullity petition.

You would have to meet all the same procedural requirements as other people, of course, and pay your share of the expenses, etc. Moreover, as far as the Church was concerned, your petition has been adjudicated and if you ever were to consider entering the Church or marrying a Catholic, the results of your case would be relevant.

Question 42:

Since our divorce, my ex and I have remained on pretty decent terms. I was wondering if perhaps we could file for an annulment of our marriage together, so that neither one of us comes across as attacking the other.

Canon law, like most legal systems, generally only allows one person to be the petitioner, and one person to be the respondent. Unlike most other legal systems, however, canon law does not pit one side against the other, even though there is often some feeling that such is being done. Even if the parties to a canonical case disagree as to how the case should be resolved, canon law does not, strictly speaking, see them as opposed to each other so much as it sees two competing theories about how to resolve a problem, neither of which theory, however, necessarily binds the tribunal which must always act in accord with law. In any event, in most cases, it's very quickly evident to the tribunal what kinds of "terms" the parties maintain with each other.

I suppose that, if it were very important to you and your ex-spouse not to come across as trying to antagonize each other, whichever of you decides to be the petitioner could include in the petition a letter from the other spouse saying something like "I look forward to cooperating in this case, etc." But it's really not necessary.

Question 43:

I was married and divorced many years ago, and I received an annulment of that first marriage. Then I remarried and stayed married until a few years ago, when my second husband left me. We divorced, of course, and I'm ambivalent about ever getting married again. But just in case, would the fact that I already got one annulment prevent me from applying for another?

There is no canonical restriction on the number of times one can apply for an annulment. Lest that sound like *carte blanche* for "serial marriages," however, remember that canon 1077 allows the diocesan tribunal to prohibit future marriages in the Church for serious reasons. Propensity toward serial marriage would, I think, certainly qualify as serious reason. Your question doesn't suggest that kind of thinking in your case, but I mention it anyway.

Question 44:

My ex-spouse and I were married first by a justice of the peace. After a few years, when things weren't going so well, we decided to get married in the Church, thinking that maybe it would help our marriage. It didn't, and we're now divorced. Will the fact that we went through two ceremonies be held against us? Are we still eligible to apply for annulment even though we got married in the Church?

Your question implies that you and probably your former spouse were both Catholic, hence you both probably disregarded canonical form in attempting your civil marriage. That will not be "held against" you, and indeed that civil marriage shows at least some sign that neither you nor your spouse had much regard for (or understanding of?) the Church's teaching on marriage. Moreover, your "second" wedding (really, the first as far as the Church is concerned) does not prevent you from filing a nullity petition, and many marriage cases deal with exactly these kinds of situations. In a sense, though, your second ceremony complicates things.

First, had you been able to bring to the tribunal only a civil wedding, such a petition probably would have been identified as a "defect of form" case and it would probably have been eligible for expedited hearing under canon 1686. Almost certainly, such a petition would be easily proven and quickly granted.

But in having undergone a canonical wedding (assuming that is what you did when you say you got married in the Church) you have forced the tribunal to investigate not the simpler question of lack of form in your first ceremony, but the more complex questions about matrimonial capacity and consent at the time of your second. The nullity of your first, civil attempt at marriage is clear, but the tribunal will also have to investigate formally your second, canonical ceremony. Thus, it will be important that the parties and witnesses in the case speak about the second ceremony as well as the first.

Often enough, of course, the same factors which led a couple into a civil wedding are seriously damaging to basic matrimonial capacity and consent at the time of the ecclesiastical ceremony. Your case, certainly, is not an unusual one. You should just be aware that it's now somewhat more complicated, ironically, by your having made, even if belatedly, some efforts to follow Church law on marriage.

Question 45:

Before our wedding, we had a formal engagement blessing, the kind you don't see much anymore. Will the fact that we underwent that additional ceremony prevent either of us from filing for an annulment after our divorce is final?

T he delightful ceremony you refer to is not in common use these days, although it's still available (more or less under 1983 CIC 1063, n.2). To answer your question, though, no, the fact that you and your former spouse underwent an engagement ceremony does not prevent you from filing a petition of nullity in regard to that marriage. Indeed, after such a ceremony, the parties remain canonically free not to marry (1983 CIC 1062 § 2). The most that could be said about the engagement ceremony would be that it might be evidence that you and your former spouse were, at the time of the wedding, apparently trying to take additional steps to prepare well for marriage.

VI. Possible Grounds for an Annulment

Question 46:

I have been told there are "multiple grounds" in my marriage case. What are "grounds," multiple or otherwise?

"Grounds" in an annulment case are like "causes of action" in a civil case or "counts" in a criminal case. The ground(s) in an annulment case are the reasons why one, or both, parties to a marriage assert that their marriage is null. Like civil causes of action or criminal counts, the mere assertion of grounds for nullity does not automatically result in nullity being declared. Grounds still have to be recognized in law, and then proven (1983 CIC 1526).

Broadly speaking, there are six ways any marriage might be proven null. First and second, it could be shown that either the husband or the wife lacked basic capacity for marriage. Third and fourth, it could be shown that either the husband or the wife did not give sufficiently his or her consent to marriage as the Church understands and proclaims it. Fifth and sixth, it could be shown that either the husband or the wife failed to manifest this consent in a proper way. None of these categories is mutually exclusive of any other category, and so two or more, or even all, of them could be present in a particular case, thus presenting multiple grounds for nullity.

More likely though, if you have been told there are multiple grounds for nullity in your case, it's because the tribunal has identified, or at least is investigating, within one or more of the above six areas, more than one specific basis for nullity. Let's take an example.

Suppose a 15 year old Catholic boy was forced at gun point to marry a 15 year old pregnant Catholic girl before a justice of the peace. Such a case offers several grounds for nullity. Assuming there was evidence to prove each of the above parts of the story, this marriage could be declared null on any, or all, of the following grounds:

(1) lack of age for the boy (canon 1083 requires Catholic men to be at least 16 years old before marrying, although Catholic girls can validly marry at 14);

(2) force and grave fear used against the boy (1983 CIC 1103);

(3) complete lack of canonical form on the part of the boy (canons 1108 & 1117 requires the Catholic boy to marry in a Catholic ceremony); and,

(4) complete lack of canonical form on the part of the girl (canons 1108 & 1117 also require Catholic girls to marry in a Catholic ceremony).

Any one of these grounds, standing completely alone, is sufficient to declare the marriage null. For that matter, other grounds for nullity could be considered as well. For example, canon 1095, n.2, requires that those entering marriage be able to exercise adequate discretion of judgment upon entering marriage. A very good case could be made that teenage boys, even over age 16, and pregnant teenage girls, even if they are over 14, do not usually exercise adequate discretion of judgment in entering any kind of marriage, let alone shotgun marriages.

Not every case, however, which offers multiple grounds for nullity is actually adjudged on each of those grounds. In the above example, it would probably be waste of time for the diocesan tribunal to adjudicate the issues related to canon 1095, which can be rather complex, when the "open-and-shut" grounds of nonage or lack of form are available. Since nullity of any type, in either party, results in nullity of the whole marriage, multiple grounds tend to be adjudicated only if those additional issues are necessary for the treatment of something besides nullity, say, in helping the tribunal address the question of imposing a *monitum* or *vetitum* on either or both parties.

This is important to understand for another reason: the mere fact that grounds were "joined," that is heard, on just one party does not necessarily imply that grounds could not have also been joined on the other party. It could simply mean that the quantity and quality of the evidence concerning the first party were more than enough to reach moral certitude of the nullity of the marriage. Likewise, that the tribunal declared nullity on the basis of one capacity, consent, or form issue does not mean that there weren't other issues seriously affecting the marriage. It just means that such additional issues, if they existed, were not needed to prove the nullity of the marriage.

Question 47:

Is pregnancy at the time of the wedding grounds for an annulment?

No. Pregnancy at the time of marriage or, for that matter, premarital sex, is not an impediment to marriage. Therefore, all things being equal, persons in these circumstances still have the canonical capacity to marry. Nevertheless, premarital sex and resulting pregnancies can, in some cases, adversely affect the consent of the parties to a marriage.

For all the reasons the Church has untiringly explained, premarital sex is not a good preparation for Christian marriage. Pregnancy, moreover, can bring with it additional physical, emotional, and financial issues which might interfere with the prayer, planning, and honest reflection which ought to be part of the marriage decision process. These additional factors can impair one's ability to deliberate and choose freely, sometimes resulting in a wedding that is a reaction to circumstances rather than a manifestation of the couple's commitment to Christian marriage. If the tribunal determines that the stressors resulting from the pregnancy and/or other related factors were such as to preclude sufficient consent to marriage as the Church understands and proclaims it, nullity can be declared.

Question 48:

My wife had a two-month affair with one of the men where she works. Is her infidelity grounds for an annulment?

Infidelity is a serious violation of the exclusive unity between husband and wife which is an essential property of marriage (1983 CIC 1056). Objectively, infidelity is gravely sinful and it qualifies as a basis for canonical separation (cf. 1983 CIC 1151–1155). Infidelity is not, however, grounds for an annulment because, standing alone, it does not prove the failure of matrimonial capacity, consent, or form, which proof is required in every annulment case.

Under certain circumstances, though, it might be that infidelity, while wrong in itself, is also evidence (though not complete proof) that another condition is present and was present at the time of the wedding, which other condition might be so destructive of matrimonial capacity or consent that it could serve as the basis for an annulment (for example 1983 CIC 1095 or 1101). In such a case, however, it's the alleged lack of capacity for, or failure of consent to, marriage in the first place which must be proven with moral certitude, and not merely the fact of infidelity.

Question 49:

Is my ex-spouse's alcoholism grounds for an annulment?

Alcoholism, whether as a professionally verified condition or, more generically, as a pattern of life with fairly obvious and consistent signs, is not a canonical impediment to marriage (cf. 1983 CIC 1083–1094) and therefore it cannot serve as the basis upon which nullity is declared.

On the other hand, active, unaddressed alcoholism, perhaps referred to as full-blown alcoholism, is obviously a very serious condition which, upon verification, could serve as the basis for the diocesan tribunal concluding that, at the time of the wedding, either or both (alcoholic) parties could not assume the essential obligations of married life for reasons of a psychic nature (*causas naturae psychicae*) as described in canon 1095, n.3. That, in turn, could be the basis of nullity in such a marriage. This is not just a word game, however, and I repeat that mere demonstration of alcoholism is not, and cannot be under canon law as it currently reads, a basis for matrimonial nullity. Consider: most reformed or recovering alcoholics describe themselves as alcoholics. One would be hard-pressed to conclude, however, that such people, as a class, are incapable of marriage.

Active alcoholism which does not manifest itself until several years into a marriage is less likely to serve as the basis of nullity under canon 1095, n.3, although the petitioner (and/or the respondent, for that matter) would be allowed to introduce evidence that the same factors which contributed to the later active alcoholism also prevented the assumption of matrimonial obligations at the time of the wedding. It is a higher burden of proof, if you will, but it could be argued. By the way, many tribunals require the testimony of an expert in hearing cases under canon 1095, n.3, but there are some cases whose fact patterns are so patent and so grave that the calling of an expert in such cases would be superfluous (1983 CIC 1574). Moreover, everything said in answer to this question about alcoholism would probably apply in cases of any chemical addiction.

Where, however, one does not claim, or cannot prove, active drug addiction or alcoholism in a clinical sense of the term, evidence of chronic drug and alcohol abuse is often raised for its relevance to one or both parties' levels of maturity and discretion of judgment in entering marriage, that is, in cases turning upon canon 1095, n.2. Finally, it is possible that drug or alcohol abuse or addiction could be used as evidence of other types of canonical nullity, for example, simulation (1983 CIC 1101).

Question 50:

When I got married, I needed to get a dispensation because my ex-husband was not baptized. I got the dispensation, but later we were divorced and we've gone our separate ways. I've been thinking about applying for annulment, and someone told me it would be an easier case because my marriage was not a sacrament. I don't understand this because we were married in a Catholic church by a Catholic priest.

I t is true that a marriage between a Christian, even a Catholic, and a nonbaptized person it not a sacrament (1983 CIC 1055 § 2), but it's still presumed to be a valid marriage and hence benefits from all of the canons which uphold marriage (1983 CIC 1060, etc.). The fact that you apparently received the necessary dispensation from the impediment of "disparity of cult" (1983 CIC 1086 § 1) also supports that presumption. Your case, despite its being a non-sacramental marriage, still must meet all the canonical requirements which face other nullity petitions in diocesan tribunals. It will be neither easier nor harder to adjudicate.

By the way, there is some chance that your case could also be considered as a "Favor of the Faith" case which is different from a Pauline Privilege situation. Favor of the Faith cases are heard only in Rome, even though they are prepared by the local tribunal. An explanation of them is beyond the scope of this work, but you might ask your tribunal about it. They will probably be able to tell you very quickly if you are not eligible to consider it.

Question 51:

My former spouse has filed for an annulment, and I believe he is planning to use my infertility, which we did not know about before our wedding, as the basis of his annulment. I feel this is terribly unfair. Please advise.

While your former spouse is basically allowed to suggest the basis, or "grounds," for an annulment case (1983 CIC 1504, n.2), he cannot dictate the grounds to the tribunal, which retains the right and duty to decide upon what basis the case will be heard (1983 CIC 1513). In any event, infertility, as opposed, say, to impotence or frigidity (1983 CIC 1084), is not a canonical basis for nullity. If that really is the sole basis upon which your former spouse can try to impugn your marriage, the petition will fail, assuming it's even accepted, which is not likely (1983 CIC 1505 § 2, n.4).

Question 52:

Our wedding was not celebrated in a Mass. Is that grounds for an annulment?

Your question suggests that you and/or your spouse were Catholic at the time of your wedding, but that for whatever reason you chose not to have a nuptial Mass. Although canonical form for the marriages of Catholics must usually be followed (1983 CIC 1117), a nuptial Mass is not required as part of that form, and hence is not required for the validity of a marriage (cf. 1983 CIC 1108 & 1118–1119). Therefore, the mere fact that a Mass was not celebrated at the time of your wedding would not serve as grounds for an annulment.

Question 53:

When I was growing up, my family moved frequently and, as a result, I was never in a parish long enough to get confirmed. No one asked me about this when I got married, but now I have heard that Catholics must be confirmed before getting married. Will this oversight affect my nullity petition?

A lmost certainly not. While the sacrament of confirmation is necessary for full Christian initiation (cf. 1983 CIC 842 § 2 & 879), it's not required for the validity of Catholic marriage. Even canon 1065 § 1, which exhorts Catholics to receive confirmation prior to getting married, only recommends reception of confirmation if it can be done "without serious inconvenience." Nowhere does canon law imply that confirmation is necessary for the validity of marriage (cf. 1983 CIC 10).

By the way, canon 1065 § 2 goes on to recommend reception of the sacraments of penance and Holy Eucharist prior to getting married, but again, as a pastoral suggestion, and not as a canonical requirement.

About the only other way in which the failure to receive confirmation might be relevant in a nullity case would be if it were offered as evidence of the "formal defection from the Church," referred to in canon 1117, which in turn might affect one's being bound by canonical form. The mere failure to receive confirmation, however, is never accepted as proof of such defection.

VII. Questions from and about the Former Spouse

Question 54:

Will my ex be notified of my request for an annulment?

Canon law requires that every effort be made to notify, or "cite," the other spouse in a petition for nullity (1983 CIC 1507 & 1620). Beyond serving legal fairness, it's usually also true that the former spouse can offer additional information about the marriage which can help the tribunal arrive at an accurate picture of the situation. The cooperation of the former spouse, therefore, is highly desirable. However, his or her refusal to participate will not preclude the tribunal from hearing a petition (1983 CIC 1510 & 1592). Indeed, under certain circumstances, the refusal of a respondent (or a petitioner, for that matter) to answer legitimate questions can be held against him or her (1983 CIC 1531 § 2). Canon law, unlike civil law, allows tribunal judges to form reasonable conclusions about why a person might refuse to answer certain questions.

Question 55:

Will my ex know what I've written or stated about our marriage?

The general rule is that both parties have the right to review all those parts of the acts of the case which will figure in the final decision, but this answer requires some nuances.

Canon 1598 § 1 protects the basic right of both parties to have an opportunity to review all the information in a case which is not already known to the parties. Other canons (cf., for example, 1983 CIC 1604 § 1) forbid extra-judicial attempts to supply information to judges or otherwise to influence the outcome of cases in such a way that the other party is unaware of the attempts.

But these canons, wise as they are, do not exist in a vacuum. Canon 1598 § 1, in fact, allows judges to withhold certain parts of the acts of the case from one or both parties if the judge fears that serious dangers are involved in disclosing the information, provided always that the right of defense remains intact despite withholding certain information. For example, a judge could withhold certain information from one of the parties and yet still protect that party's right of defense by, say, asking other questions which would address, without betraying, the matter withheld from disclosure.

Another aspect of informational access is important here: not all of the information presented in a tribunal case is necessary for the diocesan tribunal to reach its decision. One has less right to review such superfluous information. For example, in a case dealing with active drug addiction at the time of the wedding, evidence on drug abuse would certainly be important to adjudication of the case and, under normal circumstances, it would be made available to both parties. On the other hand, evidence about, say, infidelity might not be relevant to the tribunal, and could, for serious cause, conceivably be withheld from the acts of the case, provided that the judge(s) did not use the evidence of infidelity in deciding that the marriage was null due to factors related to serious drug abuse.

It is important always to recall that nullity cases are not designed to find fault or cast blame on either or both parties, and diocesan tribunals constantly struggle against being dragged into "he said/she said" squabbles, frequently enough, ones left over from the divorce. It is not relevant to the tribunal's work whether, for example, the car which one party got from the civil divorce was a lemon or was in decent shape, and such information is frequently ignored by the tribunal. Most marriage cases are processed without either party asking to know what the other said.

If such a request for review is made and granted, however, the inspection of the acts must be conducted within what will strike most Americans as rather stringent rules. There are too many canons to cite here, but these rules usually include having to review the acts only at the tribunal office during business hours and under the supervision of a tribunal official, not being allowed to make copies of or notes on the materials reviewed, not being allowed to discuss materials reviewed with anyone besides tribunal officers, and sometimes, not even being able to review the materials personally but instead only through one's canonical advocate.

If, in the end, a party truly feels that their right of defense has been improperly curtailed by the tribunal's policy on the inspection of the acts, he or she can offer that as part of an appeal under canon 1628.

Question 56:

Since our divorce, I have deliberately kept my ex-husband from finding out where I live. If I file my case, will the tribunal tell him where I live?

Tribunals gather information, they generally do not disperse it. There is no canonical requirement that respondents know the address of petitioners, and hence that kind of information is not typically shared. You should alert the tribunal to any special concerns you might have, though, about this kind of matter. Your former spouse's right of defense, moreover, always remains intact, and generally respondents have the right to review the evidence, no matter what its sources, which would be used to declare the marriage null (1983 CIC 1598).

Question 57:

My divorce was based in part on the extreme violence of my ex-husband. I'm very afraid of what might happen if he learns about my annulment. What can I do to protect myself from this happening?

Bring this concern to the attention of the diocesan tribunal at, though preferably before, the time of filing your petition. Canon law is very strict about the rights of respondents to be informed of nullity proceedings and to participate in them if they wish (1983 CIC 1511). But there are, in very exceptional circumstances, ways to deal with the problem you have suggested.

Before anything else, though, the tribunal will have to verify your claims. Many more allegations on this point are made than are verified. Evidence such as police reports, restraining orders, even medical files, can be used to support your claim. In some cases, tribunals are able to approach respondents about nullity petitions in a pacifying manner, explaining what is, and what is not, involved in the process. This might defuse problems before they ever arise.

In very difficult cases, though, only two choices will really remain: First, using the idea that no one is bound to the impossible, including the morally impossible, the tribunal could consider decreeing the respondent "morally uncitable" and proceed to hear the case. Even this will not prevent the respondent from finding out about the annulment, however. For example, notification of the annulment is always sent to the parties' church(es) of baptism for entry on the baptismal register. The respondent could request a copy of that record anytime. Or, if the petitioner later marries in the Church, the respondent could hear of the wedding and conclude that an annulment was granted, to say nothing of one's ability simply to check civil marriage records for evidence of a second marriage. Given, moreover, that marriage cases, because they deal with one's status in the Church, can always be re-opened by, say, a respondent who feels that his or her rights of defense were not respected (1983 CIC 1643), there is usually little to be gained by trying to proceed without citation of a locatable respondent.

Second, though, if the tribunal concludes that the failure to cite the respondent really will threaten the validity of the entire proceedings, but the petitioner remains adamantly, albeit reasonably, opposed to citation, the tribunal will probably recommend withdrawal of the whole petition, at least until another better time. Petitioners, in turn, have the right to appeal the refusal of the tribunal to accept a petition under those conditions (1983 CIC 1505 § 4).

Question 58:

Since my divorce, my ex-husband has consistently been late with his child support payments. He has now filed for an annulment, because he wants to get married again. I'm willing to consider cooperating with the annulment, but only if the Church orders him to get caught up on his support payments. What are my chances of getting such an order from the tribunal?

Next to nil. And not because Church officials don't sympathize with you and thousands in your situation. It's just that child support payments are one of a myriad of consequences to modern divorce which are considered by canon law to involve the "civil effects of marriage" and hence fall outside the jurisdiction of the diocesan tribunal (1983 CIC 1672). Strictly speaking, by the way, the annulment does not depend on your cooperation anyway, so you cannot use the tribunal process as leverage against your husband, no matter how deserving of help you might be.

That said, I would still recommend that you inform the tribunal about your problem for two reasons. First, such behavior might (I say might) be indicative of immaturity and irresponsibility that would be relevant to assessing your husband's matrimonial consent in the first place.

Second, canon 1071 § 1, n.3, requires priests and deacons to get a local ordinary's permission prior to celebrating the marriage of one who is bound by certain obligations toward former spouses or children. By alerting the tribunal that there might be a problem in this regard, you might (again, I say might) influence them toward placing a *monitum* or *vetitum* on your former husband's plans to remarry in the Church (1983 CIC 1077) until certain matters are addressed.

Question 59:

My ex-wife is long gone. How will that affect my marriage case if the tribunal can't find her?

The tribunal must make every reasonable effort to locate the respondent in a marriage case (1983 CIC 1508 § 1, etc.), and your cooperation in trying to locate the respondent will be important. The 1917 Code had several canons on acceptable methods of citation in cases involving absent or hard-to-find respondents (cf. 1917 CIC 1711–1725) including accepting the citation of family members and posting of notices on the doors of the tribunal, etc.

The 1983 Code, however, has dropped most of those regulations, and now merely states that citation must be done in accord with diocesan policies (1983 CIC 1509). Therefore, as long as citation methods respect a respondent's natural rights to notice, diocesan tribunals can and do vary among themselves as to steps to be followed in citing absent or hard-to-find respondents. Your own tribunal will advise you as to how much effort will be required in such cases.

Your concern, though, probably has to do with what happen in the event that, despite everyone's best efforts, the respondent simply cannot be located. In that case, most diocesan tribunals will issue something like a "decree of whereabouts unknown," declaring the respondent unlocatable, and allowing the case to proceed. In such cases, the tribunal is more likely to appoint an advocate for the respondent (1983 CIC 1481, although it is still not strictly required to do so) and one can also expect the Defender of the Bond to consider the effects an absent respondent might have had on the case. In the end, however, a nullity case can still be heard with an unlocatable respondent, and a decision can be rendered.

Question 60:

My ex-husband has gotten two letters from the tribunal, but he told me he has thrown both of them away, saying it's "my problem." Will his refusal to cooperate affect my case?

It will probably slow your case down some, but it will not, standing alone, cause it to fail. First, canon 1510 states that a respondent who refused to accept a citation is considered to have been cited. Second, assuming the diocesan tribunal can show that respondent was cited, canon 1592 allows the judge to declare a recalcitrant respondent absent from the proceedings, and to go forward with the case. Indeed, if a legitimately cited party refuses to answer questions from the tribunal, it's up to the judge(s) to decide what can be drawn from that refusal (1983 CIC 1531 § 1). While not every refusal to answer need be construed against the party refusing, neither is it a great leap to recall that people are less inclined to answer questions when they fear that they will appear to be at fault.

It may seem obvious, but it's worth repeating that diocesan tribunals really do want and value the participation of respondents. They were there, they know what happened in a marriage, and in as many cases as not, they are at least as able as petitioners to provide important information to the tribunal as it adjudicates the case. I recommend, in any event, your telling the tribunal about your ex-spouse's reaction to their letters. The tribunal need not accept your word standing alone, but your report would be noted.

Question 61:

My ex-husband suffered from mental problems all through our marriage. After our divorce he was committed to an institution. Will that pose a problem in my annulment case?

P robably not. Assuming that the diocesan tribunal can obtain jurisdiction in the case following the usual canons (1983 CIC 1673 & 105 § 2), the only difference would be that your former spouse will apparently need and be accorded a "curator," that is, one to look after his ecclesial rights (1983 CIC 1478 § 4 & 1479) and, almost certainly, a canonical advocate will be appointed by the tribunal (1983 CIC 1481 § 1). In general, persons of diminished capacity retain all of the regular procedural rights and duties of other people, and reasonable accommodation should be offered to facilitate the exercise of those rights and duties.

Question 62:

My former wife has filed for an annulment, but I want to fight it, because I know we had a valid marriage. What can I do?

First, recognize that you, the respondent, are very important in the adjudication of an annulment case, and that you have numerous rights in the process which must be respected. Indeed, the failure to respect your rights can result in the invalidity of the whole case (1983 CIC 1620, n.7).

Second, recognize that you are not being attacked, no matter what the circumstances of the marriage and divorce. It is your marriage which is being impugned, not you, and not your former spouse. There are times when the truth of this statement might not be felt, especially if grounds are joined on your possible canonical incapacity for marriage, your possible failure to consent adequately to marriage as the Church understands and proclaims it, or your possible failure to observe canonical form if it was required.

Third, participate in the case. Respond truthfully and completely when the tribunal asks for information, and know in advance that most diocesan tribunals will try to be more accommodating of respondents' concerns and schedules than they are of petitioners'. Why? Well, if for no better reason, tribunals know that petitioners want something from them, and hence petitioners are likely to be more flexible in working with the tribunal's needs; respondents, on the other hand, often don't want anything from the tribunal (except fair treatment), but respondents' co-operation can greatly facilitate what the tribunal needs to do, namely, reach an accurate decision. Besides, mistakes made in the treatment of respondents are more likely to cast doubt on the canonical force of the tribunal's decision than are mistakes made in the treatment of petitioners.

Don't, on the other hand, mistakenly conclude that, if the respondent's contribution is so important in an annulment case, the withholding of that cooperation will only hurt the petitioner's chances of getting the annulment. Wrong. It is quite possible, and it often happens, that more than enough evidence of canonical nullity is adduced even without a respondent's cooperation. Indeed, a respondent's (or a petitioner's, for that matter) failure to cooperate in a case can be held against him or her (1983 CIC 1531 § 2). There is no such thing as a Fifth Amendment in canon law.

There are, of course, many other ways to oppose an annulment. To take just one example, if the tribunal asks you to name witnesses who can, as it were, testify on your behalf, name them. And if the tribunal doesn't ask you for witnesses (which would be unusual, though not technically illegal under canon 1553), propose them anyway. Make sure the tribunal knows that you are serious about wanting your side of the story heard.

In the end, though, all of these other ways of opposing an annulment are much better explained in concrete cases by your own canonical advocate. Respondents (as well as petitioners) have the right to use a qualified canonical advocate (1983 CIC 1481 § 1) and diocesan tribunals are encouraged to keep advocates available for parties especially in marriage cases (1983 CIC 1490). While it's not precisely determined in canon law just when the right to a canon lawyer becomes operative (although it's certainly no later the "joinder of issues" discussed in canon 1513–1516, which is still early enough to be effective in most cases), an actual request for a canon lawyer made at almost any stage of the proceedings is likely to be honored by the tribunal for all of the reasons suggested above.

Remember, finally, that every canonical case is designed to identify the truth of the matter, not necessarily to grant victory to one or the other party. If you are committed to finding the truth of the situation in accord with canon law and no matter what the outcome, your participation in an annulment case is much more likely to contribute to an accurate decision by the tribunal.

Question 63:

I don't trust American tribunals. Can I request that my annulment case be heard by the tribunal in Rome?

Y ou can request it, but that doesn't necessarily mean your request is going to be honored. If you have already been cited by the diocesan tribunal, that tribunal is allowed to continue processing the case unless and until informed otherwise by Rome (cf. 1983 CIC 1417 § 2 & 1512, n.2). The summoning of a case to Rome is rare, but it might be ordered if, for example, serious malfeasance with irreparable harm were being plausibly asserted against the local tribunal. As is true of most legal systems, though, higher canonical courts tend not to interfere in the operation of lower courts, since so many early fears of litigants prove to be unwarranted when their case is actually heard. Besides, the right of appeal for all parties is protected by canon law (1983 CIC 1628), so there is time enough for higher tribunals, including Rome's, to get involved if necessary.

If you have not yet actually been cited by the local tribunal, your chances of having your case heard in Rome are somewhat better (1983 CIC 1417 § 1 & 1444), but still unlikely.

Question 64:

A few months back, I received a letter from my local diocese asking if I had any objections to a diocese in another state hearing my ex-wife's annulment case. I wrote back saying I was opposed to an annulment in any diocese. Now I get a letter from the other tribunal telling me they are hearing her case and asking if I would like to participate. Don't these people get the message? I don't want an annulment, period. How can I stop this from proceeding?

You can't block your ex-wife's petition. And both dioceses probably understood your message very clearly. My guess is that you did not understand *their* question(s).

You were not being asked whether you wanted an annulment, or whether you would agree to one, or whether you would consent to or cooperate in the process. You were asked, I am sure, whether you had any objections to the out-of-state diocese hearing your former spouse's case, in accord with canon 1673, n.3. That's all.

You wrote back and expressed your opposition to any annulment, anywhere, anytime, which you are free to do, and which response will doubtless be noted. But you did not say anything which suggested a reasonable basis for the judicial vicar of your diocese to reject the lawful request of the other diocese to hear your former spouse's petition. Apparently, that permission was thereafter granted, and the other diocese is proceeding with the case. Note, even if you had said something that looked like a plausible basis for rejecting the request, your judicial vicar would not have necessarily been bound to uphold your objection, although your chances would have been better.

In any case, the out-of-state diocesan tribunal is, almost certainly, proceeding correctly in accord with canon law. That is why you are now being asked by it to participate in the case, even though your opposition to the annulment remains as strong as ever. Remember, canon law favors the upholding of marriages (1983 CIC 1060, 1526 & 1608 § 4). Your marriage cannot be declared null unless it can be proven to have been null from the beginning. The case will be heard without you if necessary (1983 CIC 1592–1593), but it would much better for all concerned to have your input.

Question 65:

I just got the shock of my life. I got a letter from the Church telling me my marriage of over 20 years, which ended in divorce a few years ago, has been annulled. This is the very first I've heard about this. Why wasn't I asked to be involved? What can I do about this?

What you've described is extremely rare, but it can happen. Canon law insists that great efforts be made to include respondents in nullity cases and that ample measures be taken to protect their rights even if they are absent from the proceedings (1983 CIC 1511 & 1592–1593). Whatever tribunal(s) heard your case, they would have kept records of the efforts made to contact you. It is possible, though, that mistake, or fraud, kept you from being notified in a timely manner.

What to do now depends somewhat on what exactly you were told in your letter, that is, it depends somewhat on just where in the total canonical process your case is. Contact the tribunal that wrote to you and tell them what you told me. Stay calm in doing it, because diocesan tribunals not infrequently get complaints like yours from people who in fact knew what was going on all along, but who didn't take things seriously until they got a letter telling them the annulment had been declared.

You will probably be asked to help the tribunal identify just how it was that you did not receive canonical notice until so late in the process. Considering that diocesan tribunals feel as badly as people like you do in cases like this (not to mention that such a scenario raises doubts about the validity of the decision under canon 1620, n.7), they will probably bend over backward to set things right. If, however, at any point you do not feel that you are being treated fairly or honestly by the tribunal, contact independent canonical counsel for guidance and help.

VIII. Questions from and about Witnesses in an Annulment Case

Question 66:

Will I be allowed to name witnesses in my marriage case?

B asically, yes. In almost all cases, both the petitioner and the respondent are asked to name witnesses, although the mere fact one, or even both, parties have named a particular witness does not mean that the tribunal must hear that witness (1983 CIC 1547). Moreover, the tribunal can call witnesses of its own choosing but, except in cases requiring expert testimony (1983 CIC 1574–1575), this is usually not done. Respondents tend to be somewhat less likely than petitioners to name witnesses and this is not considered unusual.

Question 67:

What kinds of questions am I, or my witnesses, likely to be asked if I file my marriage case?

B ecause nullity cases are mostly concerned with the condition and circumstances of the parties at and before the time of the wedding, most of the questions will be designed to illuminate that period of time for the tribunal. That is not to say, however, that there will be no questions about the actual progress and demise of the marriage, for there certainly will be.

Questions tend to be opened-ended, inviting longer rather than shorter responses. As a practical matter, and unlike civil courts, the parties and witnesses in canonical nullity cases are usually encouraged to offer whatever information they think useful, instead of narrowly limiting themselves to direct responses to carefully crafted questions. Indeed, "yes-no" answers to tribunal questions are rarely helpful.

No area of personal life is out of bounds for questions, if that is what you are wondering about. While tribunals have no prurient desire to delve into private, including sexual, matters, where that is relevant to the issues posed to the tribunal, they will be inquired on.

For the most part, questions posed to witnesses generally track those posed to the parties. Sometimes, of course, both parties and witnesses are asked to respond to additional, more specific questions which might have occurred as result of the "instruction," or investigation of the case (1983 CIC 1570).

Witnesses are usually asked to swear or affirm the truthfulness of their answers (1983 CIC 1562). The canonical preference is that witnesses be interviewed at the tribunal offices (1983 CIC 1558 § 1) but this is often impractical and not necessary in order to obtain reliable testimony. Generally, witnesses are interviewed alone, and only in exceptional circumstances are other persons, such as the Defender of the Bond, present for the interview (1983 CIC 1560–1561).

Question 68:

What kinds of people make good witnesses?

The best witnesses in marriage nullity cases are knowledgeable, honest, and articulate. It does little good to name as a witness someone who, for example, knew you or your former spouse for only a few months toward the end of your marriage. At the risk of over-simplifying, the tribunal is not concerned about how your marriage ended, but rather with how it started. Witnesses should be able to speak about you and/or your former spouse prior to and at the time of the wedding.

Thus considered, parents generally make pretty good witnesses. In my experience, mothers are more likely to give useful overviews of one or both spouses' youth and courtship, whereas fathers tend to answer only the more direct questions. So be it, most tribunals recommend the naming of both parents (including step-parents) as witnesses. Siblings often make excellent witnesses, because their experiences often closely track those of the parties. Siblings also seem to be less likely to "interpret" their testimony than some parents (who might feel that their performance in raising their children is being indirectly questioned by a nullity case) seem to be. Most tribunals encourage and readily accept sibling testimony.

Best men and maids of honor are often named as witnesses, but somehow they tend not to be as useful as one might think. The friends of youth see only with the eyes of youth, and in a mobile society such as ours, these earlier friends often lose touch with each other and the parties. Still, the tribunal might well ask for them, so listing them will save time in most cases. Other friends from that period of time can be named as well, of course.

In recommending that witnesses be honest, one need not imply that witnesses lie to Church tribunals, although they do, every day. Rather, the suggestion is that people who are less likely to shade their testimony, as well as people whose general life style shows maturity and integrity, be named as witnesses. For example, in a case turning on questions of pre-wedding drug or alcohol abuse, the naming of former, but unreformed, drug buddies might not accomplish much, for such witnesses are often motivated to minimize their, and the party's, drug or alcohol involvement. On the other hand, reformed alcoholics tend to be very honest and accurate about levels of substance abuse. What the tribunal needs are honest, accurate reports.

Finally, witnesses who are more likely to be articulate should be named. This quality is, in some cases, hard to predict, but it should be considered, for many petitions stall, or fail, because the witnesses offer only a short series of "yes-no" answers to questions requiring much more careful thought. You should know that most tribunals will accommodate a w itness's request to be interviewed rather than filling out a questionnaire, or will allow them to respond in writing if travel to the tribunal offices is difficult. Similarly, tribunals are to make special efforts to accommodate witnesses whose first language is not English (1983 CIC 1471).

If, during the investigation of your case, problems develop because the poor quality of witness testimony, you will probably be contacted and asked to name additional witnesses. Such requests are often a sign that the case is stalling, and might well be the last attempt a tribunal will make to move the case toward resolution.

Of course, if the testimony which comes in is canonically reliable, but it points to validity of the marriage, so be it. The tribunal is dedicated to the truth of the situation, not necessarily in saying yes to every nullity petition it gets. In the end, you can only do the best you can do. You name the best witnesses you can find, and then you let the tribunal process take its course.

Question 69:

Will my children be called as witnesses if I file a nullity petition?

S trictly speaking, anyone above the age of 14 is considered eligible to testify before a diocesan tribunal, and in some cases children even younger than that could be called (1983 CIC 1550). But most tribunals avoid calling children as witnesses in the marriage cases of their parents for several reasons.

First, marriage cases are concerned primarily with facts and circumstances prior to and at the time of the wedding. In most marriages, of course, there were no children at the time of the wedding, but that is changing as more cases of divorce in "blended" families, with older children present during and before the impugned marriage, come before diocesan tribunals for adjudication. Still, in most cases, children could not testify because they were not around at the times most relevant to the tribunal's inquiry.

A second obstacle to calling children as witnesses lies in the fact that either party can request the exclusion of a witness based on "just cause" (1983 CIC 1555). One party or the other might well offer just causes as to why children should not be called as witnesses in the nullity cases of their parents. A tribunal would be hard put not to honor such a request by either or both parties although, strictly speaking, it's not bound by such requests. Moreover, judges are to curb excessive numbers of witnesses (1983 CIC 1553), and it would be easy for a judge to decide that child witnesses are "excessive" in most cases.

In brief, the calling of children, especially younger children, as witnesses in a marriage case is rare, but it's not impossible. If you still have concerns about this, bring them to your advocate's, or the tribunal's, attention, as soon as possible.

Question 70:

Will I be allowed to name my therapist as a witness in my annulment case?

You may list your therapist as a witness, but it will be up to the tribunal to decide whether the therapist will be contacted (1983 CIC 1547, 1575 & 1581), even though you should expect to pay any fees which might be charged by your therapist for testifying. Several factors will influence the tribunal's decision on calling an expert your suggest.

The type(s) of therapist(s) you list will make a difference in whether he or she is called as a witness. For example, a psychiatrist will more likely be able to give the tribunal the kind of technical information it needs in adjudicating a marriage case than will a social or case worker, and hence would be more likely to be called upon for testimony. Similarly, therapists with special certification in, say, marriage and family life tend to be more helpful than therapists who specialize in, say, occupational adjustment disorders. On the other hand, therapists with special training in the areas of most concern to the tribunal in a given case (say, drug and alcohol counselors in a case involving substance abuse) will more likely be called as witnesses than would even a marriage and family life counselor.

Therapists with long records of involvement with one or both parties will more likely be called upon than will a therapist who knew one or both parties only briefly (typically, after the divorce, which is the least useful period for evidence gathering.). Therapists who make use of standard personality profiles and psychological/psychiatric batteries tend to be more useful to the tribunal than are therapists who do not, or cannot, administer and interpret such tests.

Therapists who have worked with diocesan tribunals in the past are more likely to be called as witnesses than those who know little or nothing about the issues with which tribunals must be concerned. This is usually a matter of efficiency.

It is not necessary that the therapist be Catholic in order to testify. Not all therapists are Catholic, of course, and not all Catholic therapists share the Church's commitment to marriage. As a tribunal judge, however, I have seen therapist reports which, deliberately or otherwise, argued about Church teaching on marriage rather than focusing on the facts of the case before them. This does no one any good.

From time to time, the tribunal itself will seek the opinion of a psychological/psychiatric expert, or other kind of expert for that matter, to help it understand the facts of a particular case. Strictly speaking, if an expert is engaged by the tribunal only to examine the evidence already presented in a case, and the party or parties are not going to be charged an additional fee for such review, the tribunal could submit the materials for the expert's review without notifying the parties in advance. This would seem to be done only rarely, however, and in any event, the parties are free to make replies to the opinions of experts (1983 CIC 1598, etc.).

Alternatively, the tribunal might suggest that one (or both) parties in a nullity case undergo an evaluation with a counselor approved by the diocesan tribunal, which counselor will then make his or her report directly to the tribunal. In these cases, the party or parties undergoing the evaluation are almost always required to pay any fees associated with such evaluations (1983 CIC 1580), and frequently the results of the evaluation are not shared with the parties afterward. This is because the expert is not attempting to serve the parties, but rather to assist the tribunal. If such an option is going to be suggested in your case, you will be notified in advance and your permission will be requested. Your consent cannot be forced by the tribunal, however, and you are free to say no. Occasionally, however, your refusal will mean that insufficient evidence of nullity will be adduced in your petition and your petition will fail.

One should be aware that civil laws on confidentiality might prevent a therapist from answering diocesan tribunal questions on one spouse without the consent of the other spouse. Such additional consent is not always provided of course, and there is little the tribunal can do to encourage it. Still, most therapists are able to answer questions about one spouse.

Note: therapists differ with regard to the length of time they will maintain client records. I have seen important questions posed to therapists, with complete consent to answer provided, only to have the therapist reply that records are no longer available.

Question 71:

I've been talking with a priest for many years about the problems in my marriage. Can I ask him to serve as a witness in my nullity petition?

That depends. If you have gone to confession to this priest and you would now like him to testify about things you brought to the confessional (perhaps as evidence that the factors which you claim eventually destroyed the marriage were present from the very beginning) the answer is absolutely no (1983 CIC 1550 § 2, n.2, 983 & 1388). This applies even if you specifically authorize the priest to relate what he heard in your confession. The Church simply will not allow anything which could even appear to jeopardize the seal of confession.

Alternatively, even if you went to confession to this priest, you might want him to relate things that you discussed outside of confession. Strictly speaking, the priest is probably canonically free to relate such information especially with your consent, but be aware that you are putting him in a very delicate position. It is, in any event, fully within the authority of the tribunal to reject such a priest as a witness, even over your objections. If the priest so much as hints that he feels the sacramental seal to be an issue in his testimony, you had better expect him to be stricken from the witness list (cf. also canon 1548 § 2, n.1, which allows clerics to avoid testifying, if they wish, on anything made known to them in connection with sacred ministry.).

Finally, however, it is possible that there is no question of the seal of confession or ministerial confidentiality being threatened if your priest advisor testifies. In such cases you are free to name the priest as a witness, and the tribunal can exercise its normal discretion in calling, or not calling, the priest. Personally, however, I find parish priests to be rather weak as witnesses in marriage cases. Most of their information tends to come from just one spouse in a troubled marriage, their contact with troubled couples usually does not significantly pre-date the wedding, and they are generally so busy with other things that what they know and say tends to be, from a canonical point of view at least, rather superficial. Occasionally, of course, a priest witness overcomes all of these short-comings, and he serves the tribunal's needs well. But as a general rule, I advise against naming priests as witnesses in nullity cases.

Question 72:

I can't think of any witnesses for my marriage case. What can I do?

That is a serious problem, and it could result in the failure of your petition, but it's not the virtually insurmountable problem it used to be.

Because marriage cases are, understandably, considered to deal with the public good (1983 CIC 1691), certain special rules apply to them, including a rule which says that, standing alone, the mere declaration of a party cannot be accepted as full proof on a point (1983 CIC 1536 § 2). While the tribunal judge(s) can work with a party to try to adduce additional evidence (1983 CIC 1530 & 1452 § 2), at least some other corroboration of the petitioner's claim will have to be forthcoming before a tribunal could even think about reaching moral certitude of nullity (cf. 1983 CIC 1060 & 1608 § 4).

For that matter, in most cases, the testimony of a single witness (as distinguished from a party) on any given point is also usually not considered full proof of that point (1983 CIC 1573). But here is where the 1983 Code is somewhat more lenient in its norms on the interpretation of evidence than was the 1917 Code. Canon 1573 of the 1983 Code, for example, does allow the testimony of a single witness to carry a point if, fairly considered, the general circumstances suggest such testimony to be credible. It is up to the judge(s) to assess those circumstances (1983 CIC 1572).

Moreover, even if the only evidence on a point comes from the declaration of the petitioner or respondent, the 1983 Code allows such declarations to carry probative weight if they amount to what canon law considers a "judicial confession" against the party himself or herself (1983 CIC 1535 & 1536). People tend not to want to admit faults or flaws in themselves, so canon law is willing to give some higher credence to statements made by a party which reflect poorly on that party. On the other hand, tribunal judges, to say nothing of Defenders of the Bond, will understandably look carefully at petitioner or respondent declarations which suddenly, and conveniently, seem filled with admissions which, however poorly they reflect on the party making them, also make it more likely that the annulment petition will be granted. The

Church is all in favor of growth in self-knowledge and the free admission of personal faults and flaws; it just wants those admissions to be accurate.

The tribunal will usually work with the parties to help them uncover witnesses, but it will not do the parties' work for them. The burden of proof is on you, the petitioner, in a marriage case (1983 CIC 1526). While going into a marriage case with few or no witnesses is not the nearly insurmountable obstacle it used to be, doing so makes it less likely that the tribunal will be able to reach moral certitude of nullity.

Question 73:

Last year a couple with whom my husband and I have been friends for many years got divorced. My husband and I were named as witnesses in a nullity case filed by one of them. We very much want to avoid taking sides in this tragic affair. On the other hand, we want to cooperate with the Church, if we really ought to. Please advise.

Your concern is a common one, but it usually grows out of a misunderstanding of how canon law in general, and marriage nullity cases in particular, are conducted. Although both parties in a canonical nullity case can name witnesses, it's up to the tribunal to decide which witnesses are actually called (1983 CIC 1547). You have been notified, therefore, not so much that one side or the other wants your help in arguing their case, but that the diocesan tribunal wants your help in making an informed decision.

Whether your testimony is taken in person or in writing, and regardless of who requested that you be called as a witness, you will quickly see that the tribunal's questions are not geared to helping or hurting one side or the other in a marriage case. Rather, you are being asked to describe as objectively as possible the actual facts and circumstances of the marriage. If, in fact, this reflects better or worse on one of the parties, so be it. It often happens that witnesses suggested by one party end up giving testimony about that party which is unflattering. Again, that is normal and acceptable. In any event, as a witness you are not being asked to take sides or to determine whether either or both parties "deserve" an annulment. You are being asked, by the tribunal, for information which the tribunal needs to make an accurate decision.

If, however, you are still concerned that your participation in a case might hurt you or someone you love or that your relationship with either or both parties might suffer (and you have already taken into consideration that your failure to participate might do the very same thing), there are two options open to you.

First, you can ask that your testimony be held confidential from the parties. Tribunal judges have the authority to withhold some testimony from the parties under canon 1598, but such authority is to be used only in serious cases. Hurt feelings, no matter how much they hurt, are usually not considered sufficient basis upon which to withhold information from the parties.

Second, you could invoke canon 1548 § 2, n.2, which allows persons who fear that ill-repute, dangerous problems, or other evils will be imposed on them or their loved ones in the event that they testify, to avoid testifying in a case.

But, let's be frank here: Whatever the legitimate authority of a diocesan tribunal to seek testimony from a witness (1983 CIC 1557), it has next to no power to enforce that request. The Church does not have police to arrest contumacious witnesses, and it does not have jails to put them in. If a witness really refuses to cooperate, even for unjust reasons, there isn't much the tribunal can do about it. That said, I only repeat that "fear of testifying" is often exaggerated by potential witnesses.

IX. The Effects of an Annulment

Question 74:

If one spouse gets an annulment, does it count for the other spouse as well?

Yes, by definition, it has to. An annulment is an official declaration that what appeared to be a marriage was in fact not one. Just as it takes two people to make one marriage, so one annulment means that neither of the two persons were, according to canon law, married, even if the canonical reason(s) for nullity were centered on just one of the two spouses.

Question 75:

Will an annulment decide who was to blame for our divorce?

No. The annulment process is neither designed nor intended to attribute blame or fault to one side or the other. Remember that the annulment process is the Church's way to determine as accurately as possible whether the parties in an impugned marriage were validly married in the first place. The technical issues in annulment cases are the purely canonical ones of capacity, consent, and form.

This does not mean, however, that one party can not be the focus of tribunal investigation more than the other. If grounds for nullity are more obvious, or are more easily proven, with one party than other (indeed, perhaps the other party exhibited no grounds for nullity) then that party will be the one upon whom the case is heard. Even then, fault is simply not a factor in the tribunal's treatment of the case.

That said, many people experience in the annulment process an opportunity to reflect on an important and usually stressful period in their life. In doing so, they often come to learn more about their own strengths and weaknesses. This growth in self-knowledge can help in the divorce healing process, and in some cases can help prepare one for the possibility for a future successful marriage in the Church.

Question 76:

Will an annulment render the children illegitimate?

No, but this answer requires some nuance.

First, let's say a few words on the notion of illegitimacy. It stinks. Babies are not illegitimate, no matter how illegitimate might have been the acts by which they were conceived. Babies are conceived in the image and likeness of God.

Second, illegitimacy no longer carries any canonical consequences that I can see. For example, children born illegitimate are no longer hampered in seeking ordination as they were under the 1917 Code (cf. 1917 CIC 984, n.1, as compared to 1983 CIC 1041). The only reason the concept of legitimacy is still treated in the 1983 Code is, I think, because some nations, by treaty with the Holy See, will accept canonical declarations of nullity as civil divorces, which is fine as far as that goes, but such policies could raise the possibility that post-divorce civil questions of child-support and inheritance could be clouded if legitimacy were not treated in canon law. These kinds of concerns are not relevant, however, in the United States.

Notwithstanding all the above reasons not to worry about canonical legitimacy, questions are still frequently raised about the effects of annulments on the legitimacy of children.

Canon 1137 states that children born or conceived of a valid or putative marriage are considered legitimate. Canon 1061 § 3 calls "putative" those marriages which, although invalid, were nevertheless celebrated in good faith by at least one of the parties, until that time, if any, when both parties become certain of its nullity. The great majority of the formal nullity cases coming before diocesan tribunals in fact involve at least one, usually two, persons entering marriage in good faith, hence entering at least a putative marriage, resulting in the legitimacy of the children. But there are a few exceptions to this general conclusion.

First, if a child is born less than 180 days after the canonical wedding (not the civil wedding, if there was one), he or she is not canonically presumed legitimate (1983 CIC 1138 § 2). Thus, the rushed religious wedding some people feel is necessary before the baby is born does not always result in the canonical legitimation of the child. Notice, however, that legitimacy arises from the timing of the wedding relative to the birth of the baby; it has nothing to do with the later annulment. Frankly, though, it should be admitted that canon law is behind the scientific curve here: it's not uncommon today for children to be born very immaturely, and survive. Such children fall in between a canonical crack, even if they are legitimately conceived.

On the other hand, if a child is born to parents not married or only civilly married, but then the parents later validly, or even putatively, marry, such marriage automatically renders the child or children canonically legitimate (1983 CIC 1139). Even here, though, the later annulment of the marriage does not render the children canonically illegitimate. Finally, canon 1139 states that children can be legitimated by rescript of the Holy See.

In brief, the granting of an annulment petition does nothing to affect the legitimacy of children. That status, to the scant degree it has any canonical significance, is determined prior to the time any questions of annulments are raised.

Question 77:

I have been told that even if my annulment goes through, there is still a very good chance that I would still not be allowed to remarry in the Church, that I will be prohibited from remarrying. What is this all about? Who gives them that right?

An annulment only determines that what was believed to be a valid marriage was not one as far as the Church is concerned. In reaching that conclusion, the Church states that the parties whom it earlier presumed to be bound by a marriage are not actually bound, and hence, in that respect, and in that respect only, they are free to enter marriage in the Church (cf. 1983 CIC 1085 § 1).

But it often happens that, in adjudicating a marriage case, the tribunal finds a condition which not only seriously affected one's capacity or consent at the time of the wedding, but which is clearly still at work in either (or both) of the parties. Let's take "untreated alcoholism," as an example.

If, (I say if), the active alcoholism which destroyed one's capacity or consent for marriage the first time around remains unaddressed, there is little reason to doubt its deleterious effects on marriage the second time around as well. No one wants to see that happen so, using canon 1077 § 1, the tribunal can impose a *"vetitum"* on either party (or both parties, if circumstances warrant). A *vetitum* is a prohibition against a future marriage until, in this example, the alcoholism is competently addressed. Sounds good so far, but this is where the problems start.

First, the *vetitum* can last only as long as the problem lasts. This, too, sounds reasonable, until one begins to realize that many of the factors which destroy matrimonial capacity or consent do not fit into such neat time-bound patterns whose resolution can be accurately spotted. Moreover, the canonical presumptions in favor of matrimonial capacity and consent (1983 CIC 1058 & 1101) keep pressure on Church officials to lift prohibitions sooner than later.

Second, a *vetitum* can affect only current subjects of the bishop whose tribunal issued the *vetitum* in the first place. Of course, people move from place to place over time and, while neighboring dioceses try to be respectful of each other's *vetita,* there is no strict requirement that they do so. As the years and miles accumulate, the perceptiveness achieved by the first tribunal might not be shared by the second. Furthermore, the tribunal hearing the nullity case might have had jurisdiction over the respondent only for purposes of hearing the marriage case (1983 CIC 1673, nn.1, 3, or 4), leaving little apparent basis for canon 1077 to apply.

Third, and most important, although marrying under an unresolved *vetitum* is illicit, no prohibition by a bishop or tribunal can, by itself, prevent the putative validity of such a marriage. At least three canons (1983 CIC 1075, 1076, & 1077) make it quite clear that only the pope can prohibit a given marriage upon pain of invalidity. There are, unfortunately, some cases of couples, even with the cooperation of Catholic ministers, entering marriage in violation of their prohibitions. Such scenarios, even if not automatically null, are tailor-made for disaster.

Clearly, canons 1075–1077 reflect a concern that marriage, and the faithful's right to enter marriage, could suffer abuse (deliberate or otherwise) at the hands of local Church authorities if the power to make *vetita* invalidating were given to bishops or their tribunals. On the other hand, having to stand by and watch people serially enter invalid marriages doesn't seem to serve the common good either.

Ideally, people who receive a *vetitum* during an annulment process (and they are not commonly imposed) will recognize that such a prohibition represents the dispassionate conclusion of experienced observers who only want to help. (I'm sorry if that sounds quaint, but it's true.) Meanwhile, family and friends can help by not greeting the news of an upcoming second wedding as if it's going to be an automatic cure-all for whatever went wrong the first time. It is difficult not to feel joy at a wedding announcement. But, these days especially, a little prudent reserve might be helpful too.

Question 78:

My annulment has been approved, and I just got a letter from the tribunal saying the appellate court agreed with my annulment. But the letter also said that I have a "monitum" on me and that I will have to contact the tribunal before making any marriage plans in the future. Please explain what this is all about.

I assume that when you say "*monitum*," you and the tribunal mean "*monitum*," and not "*vetitum*." A *vetitum*, for reasons given elsewhere, is frankly a more serious matter than is a *monitum*. But having said that, I don't wish to understate the importance of what you have been told.

A *monitum* is not an official canonical institution, at least not in marriage cases. Literally "a warning," notice of a *monitum* by a tribunal is just the tribunal's way of saying, in effect, "Your annulment has been granted, but we're concerned lest you rush into a another marriage before taking some time to digest what has happened and to prepare better for a successful marriage." Assuming that you and the tribunal are using the terms correctly, a *monitum* is not prohibition against a future marriage in the Church, as would be the case with a *vetitum*. Rather, a *monitum* is a friendly, if firm, suggestion by knowledgeable people that some issues raised by your first marriage and divorce should be considered, perhaps with professional help, before you enter another marriage. The tribunal will explain its precise concerns if and when you contact it.

X. If the Answer Is No

Question 79:

After four years of what I thought was a happy marriage, my ex-husband took some drugs on a bet and, within a year, he was completely addicted, unemployed, violent, and we were bankrupt. We were divorced and I applied for an annulment, which was denied! There is absolutely no way I'm going back to him. What does the Catholic Church expect me to do?

When you say your nullity petition was denied, I assume you mean you got a formal negative decision from a diocesan tribunal, and not just an opinion from them, let alone some speculation from whomever. I assume that your case was heard, that you have no reasonable basis for appeal, and that you have discussed all of this with a canonical advisor of your choosing.

That said, I am not entirely surprised by what seems to be the outcome of your case, since your description in the broadest terms paints a picture of a good marriage gone tragically bad. Marriages that die are not necessarily null; that is a fact of canon law, derived from Church teaching, in turn resting in the Truth which is Christ. Only marriages which were null from the beginning can be declared null in the end.

Now, to your question about what does the Church expect of you. Well, I can say that it does not expect you to go back to your former spouse, although strictly speaking you would be free to do that if circumstances warranted it. Generally, validly married couples have a right and duty "to preserve the conjugal life" (1983 CIC 1135 & 1151), but no one is bound to the impossible, or the dangerous, in a marriage situation (1983 CIC 1153).

Incredible as it might seem, marriages worse than the one you are describing have come back together, albeit with grace and hard work. Not many, maybe, but some. Christ makes all things new. I'm not going to gloss over damage that such conduct works on a marriage, or minimize the efforts that it can, and probably would, require to put things aright. But marriage is a sacrament for baptized couples and every sacrament is a source of strength and renewal in Christ for its recipients.

In any event, the Church does not expect anything in particular from you based on the fact of your divorce that it does not already expect of you based on your baptism and your call to holiness which remains despite your divorce. The Church does, however, expect you not to do one thing, namely, it does expect you not to attempt another marriage in the Church, since for as long as nullity cannot be proven and your former spouse is alive, you are considered bound by the marriage which you entered, and which someone else betrayed.

Question 80:

I've been told that my annulment petition will probably not be approved, but that I could apply for a Pauline Privilege. What is that and why do I qualify?

The Pauline Privilege, so named because it derives from St. Paul's writings in 1 Corinthians 7:12–15, is treated in canons 1143 and following. Basically, the tribunal is telling you that, based on a preliminary assessment of the facts of your case, you might be able to contract a new, valid marriage, even if your first marriage could not be proven null.

I'll assume your case fits the most common type of case in which the Pauline Privilege is possible. Variations between what follows and what is actually true in your case, however, would not automatically mean that your chances of using the Pauline Privilege are gone. Nor does meeting each requirement below guarantee your eligibility for the Pauline Privilege; this is only a basic guide.

1) Both you and your former spouse were not baptized at the time of your wedding. This has to be canonically proven.

2) You received Christian, not necessarily Catholic, baptism after your wedding, and your former spouse did not at any time relevant. This also has to be canonically proven.

3) Your nonbaptized, former spouse canonically "departed." Usually, this means that he or she sought a divorce for almost any reason, but strictly speaking, separation or divorce is not canonically required. Even if you filed for the civil divorce (which is permissible), you must not have been improperly the cause of the break-up. For example, you must not have committed adultery against your former spouse. It must somehow, fairly considered, be your former spouse who will not let you live your new Christian faith. You need not use the Pauline Privilege immediately upon your baptism, and continued cohabitation, including sexual relations, can be shared after baptism without prejudice to the operation of the Pauline Privilege.

4) Following a canonical investigation and verification of the above basic points (all of which can be conducted by local Church officials), you would be permitted to contract a new marriage with a Catholic, or any Christian, or even a non-baptized person. The new marriage, not your baptism, would dissolve, not annul, your first marriage.

By the way, being told (presumably by tribunal officials) that your original nullity petition "probably will not be approved" is not the same thing as getting a formal decision from them, although it might well be an informed prediction. Keep in mind, in any event, that you do have the right to a decision on the merits of your petition, if you decide to exercise those rights. Finally, you need not either exhaust the Pauline Privilege option before filing for an annulment, nor be rejected in an annulment proceeding before applying the Pauline Privilege.

Because the amount of work to be done by the tribunal in a Pauline Privilege case is almost the same as the amount of work required in a formal nullity case, most tribunals will ask for roughly the same fee in Pauline cases that they charge for formal cases. If you have questions about this, just ask.

Question 81:

If my annulment is not granted by my diocesan tribunal, can I take my case to another tribunal?

P robably, but be careful here. If your nullity petition was actually heard, but it received a negative sentence, that is, if the diocesan tribunal said no to your request, you have the right to appeal that negative decision to the next higher court (1983 CIC 1628). For practical purposes, though, you are pretty much left with having to deal with the consequences of that negative sentence in part because once a diocesan tribunal establishes jurisdiction over a case, it more or less keeps it.

Therefore, even if you were to file your case anew in another tribunal, mentioning nothing about your negative sentence from another tribunal, the second tribunal would probably be acting invalidly, albeit unwittingly, in perchance accepting the case (1983 CIC 1415 & 1512, n.2). Don't even try to deceive a diocesan tribunal about issues related to its jurisdiction. Marriage cases, because they deal with the status of persons in the Church, are canonically very easy to re-open, even without your consent (1983 CIC 1430, 1643 & 1674). Any hint of deception on these kinds of points could bring a swift tribunal response.

On the other hand, if your case was not formally heard by the diocesan tribunal, but for various reasons it does not appear that your petition can be granted, you could ask for the transfer of your case to another competent tribunal. You might be asked to withdraw formally your case from the first tribunal (1983 CIC 1524), but as long as you fully disclose the fact of the earlier filing and why you wish a new tribunal to hear your case, the second tribunal will give it a fair consideration. This is not "forum shopping" as the concept is understood in civil law and if it were, canon law itself would probably prevent you from doing it (cf., for example, 1983 CIC 1488 § 2). Transfer of cases is not a common practice, but reasons for which it might be considered (not necessarily granted, however) would include excessive backlog at the first tribunal or the relocation of either or both parties in the case to another diocese.

Question 82:

If my annulment doesn't go through, will I be prohibited from receiving the sacraments?

If you are prohibited from receiving the sacraments, it's because your marital status is already irregular, not because your annulment was not granted.

If, for example, you are divorced, but you have not since then attempted marriage outside the Church, your right to approach the sacraments is not affected at all by the mere fact of the civil divorce. I assume, therefore, that you are asking because you already are in a second marriage. That is what raises the question of your participation in the sacraments.

Divorce and remarriage outside the Church generally places one in objective grave sin and therefore prevents one from receiving the Eucharist (1983 CIC 915). For those who might doubt the interpretation of this canon on technical grounds, I would call attention to the Congregation for the Doctrine of the Faith letter on the Reception of Communion by Divorced and Remarried Catholics (14 September 1994, Para. 9), upholding this same view which is, in any event, the traditional understanding.

You can, of course, approach the sacrament of Penance at any time, if you have firm purpose of amendment (1983 CIC 980). This would imply, however, if not a separation from your new spouse (which might be impractical for any number of reasons) at least a resolution not to share those conjugal relations which are reserved for the married. You may also receive the sacrament of Anointing of the Sick under basically the same conditions (1983 CIC 1007).

I note, finally, that you did not ask about whether you were excommunicated because, I assume, you already correctly knew that divorce and remarriage outside the Church no longer results in excommunication.

XI. Miscellaneous

Question 83:

If a Catholic gets married in the Church, but then gets divorced and marries someone else civilly without an annulment, is he or she excommunicated?

Not since October 22nd, 1977, when Pope Paul VI authorized dropping the American ecclesiastical legislation (dating from the Council of Baltimore in 1884) which imposed the excommunication on the remarrying Catholic(s) in the first place. And, if there is anyone out there who divorced and remarried before 1977, they should know that the same removal of penalties applies to them as well (1983 CIC 1313 § 2). Remarriage outside the Church, however, is still objectively gravely sinful and does affect one's ability to participate in the sacraments, including the Eucharist.

Question 84:

What is an internal forum solution? It has been suggested as a possible way to work through my marriage situation.

In the marriage and divorce context, the internal forum solution is presented by some as a way of allowing divorced and remarried Catholics to approach the sacraments without first canonically resolving their irregular marital status in the Church by means of the annulment process, Pauline Privilege, etc.

Basically, the theory holds that those who cannot canonically prove the invalidity of a former marriage, sincerely believed to be invalid, should not be deprived of the sacraments after remarrying, since it's not their fault that canon law does not recognize the invalidity of that earlier marriage. Depending on who is presenting the solution, it might or might not require consultation with a priest before implementation, it might or might not require receiving sacraments at a parish where one is not known, and it even might or might not require having filed a marriage case with the diocesan tribunal, let alone having exhausted the opportunities for appeal, etc.

But, regardless of how such variations on the theme are answered, and regardless of who is presenting the solution for consideration, the internal forum solution is not a solution for Catholics laboring under canon 915 as a result of their irregular marital status. As recently as 1994, the highest levels of Church authority have deliberately and unambiguously rejected internal forum solutions in cases of irregular marriage situations (cf. Congregation for the Doctrine of the Faith, letter on Reception of Communion by Divorced and Remarried Catholics, 14 September 1994). The fact that so many Catholics are apparently using "internal forum solutions" to resolve their marital status problems based on the advice of priests and other spiritual counselors might well lessen their responsibility for having applied an inappropriate solution to their situation, but it does not make their solution correct.

Question 85:

With divorce rates so high, and many Catholics seeking annulments, what prevents a divorced couple from just making up a story in order to get their annulment? How can Church officials verify what really happened in a marriage?

Even though an annulment is a religious pronouncement, nullity petitions are still conducted in a legal context and must meet certain well established canonical requirements before being granted.

First, canon 1060 states that marriage "enjoys the favor of law." In other words, marriage, whether it be strictly Catholic, more broadly Christian, generally believing, or simply pagan, is presumed valid. A mere request for annulment is not sufficient to get one, even if both former spouses desire it. Instead, the marriage must be proved under canon law to have been invalid (1983 CIC 1526).

Moreover, not only is the marriage itself generally considered valid, but the various elements which go into a marriage are given the benefit of the doubt. For example, persons are presumed capable of marriage unless prohibited by law (1983 CIC 1058) and the consent of the mind is presumed to be in accord with the words said at the wedding (1983 CIC 1101 § 1). All of these add up to impressive burdens of proof on those who would have a marriage declared null.

Second, canon 1608 requires the tribunal, if it finds for nullity, to have reached that decision with "moral certitude." This is a canonical version, though not simply the equivalent, of the civil law standard of "beyond a reasonable doubt." Canon 1608 means that it's not enough to show that a marriage could have been null, or even that it was more likely null than not. Instead, the judge(s) must be deeply assured that nullity has been proven in accord with the requirements of canon law.

There remains, of course, as suggested by your question, the possibility of collusion between the parties. Indeed, some marriage cases stand or fall based on information known only to the parties themselves. Because the Church does not have the same kind of physical and financial resources to compel in its courts the truthfulness which is available to civil courts (but see 1983 CIC 1391 on the crime of falsehood), the Church frankly does rely rather more on the cooperation and integrity of the participants to arrive at accurate decisions. This is not as unreasonable as a cynical age might think since, in the great majority of nullity petitions, there are only religiously-inspired motives at work in the first place. But even the most sincere parties can still be mistaken regarding their evidence.

At least two additional canonical institutions serve, as it were, to monitor the accuracy of tribunal decisions. First, a Defender of the Bond participates in every nullity petition passing before a diocesan tribunal. His or her task is to make sure that all of the reasonable arguments against declaring matrimonial nullity have been considered by the tribunal. Second, again because of the seriousness with which the Church defends the value of marriage, every case in which a marriage is declared null by a diocesan tribunal is automatically appealed to a higher court, again, regardless of the opinion of the parties, or even of the Defender of the Bond (1983 CIC 1682). An entirely independent tribunal must agree that the annulment was properly granted before it becomes official.

Question 86:

I have been told that I actually need two annulments before I can get married again. But I was only married once. What is going on?

I assume that when you say you were married only once, you don't have in mind the so-called "marriage that doesn't count" situation. For reasons explained elsewhere, there's no such thing as a marriage that doesn't count, and if this is what the tribunal is concerned about in your case, then you really do need two annulments.

More likely though, what you have been told has to with do a special rule in canon law applying only to marriage cases. Briefly, every decision by a diocesan tribunal which results in a declaration of matrimonial nullity must be appealed to a higher ecclesiastical court (1983 CIC 1682 § 2). Known technically as "appeal by law," this rule applies even if both parties to the marriage wanted the annulment, and even if the Defender of the Bond had no objections to the declaration of nullity. It is, therefore, only when the higher court, known as "second instance," agrees with the first court that a marriage has been proven null, that the parties to that marriage are considered free of the marriage bond which would have otherwise arisen.

There is no additional fee for an "appeal by law" hearing and in most, but not all, cases, the first court's decision is confirmed by the higher court. If the second instance court does not agree with the first court's declaration of nullity then, depending on certain procedural facts, the case might be returned to first instance for reconsideration or either or both parties could appeal the negative decision of second instance to the Roman Rota. Those options are usually explained only in the event they are needed because of the complexities involved.

Usually a second instance process is conducted by tribunal personnel, although the parties to the marriage are informed about what is happening in the case, should they wish to take a more active part. Only in difficult cases would either or both parties be called upon to supply additional information to the higher court.

Question 87:

What is a "marriage that doesn't count"?

As the phrase usually crops up in tribunal practice, it's a seriously misleading conclusion derived from some otherwise correct canonical principles. In brief, there's no such thing as a marriage that doesn't count, but some examples might help.

Example 1: a teenaged Catholic bound by canonical form runs off to Vegas and marries before a justice of the peace. A few weeks later the couple splits up and they get a civil divorce. Several years later, though, this Catholic wishes to marry in the Church. Example 2: a Catholic, free to marry, attempts in good faith to marry someone whom, unbeknownst to the Catholic, is already validly married. The truth gets out and, to no one's surprise, a civil divorce follows quickly. Later, this Catholic wishes to marry validly.

Both of these earlier attempts at marriage are so obviously likely to be null (1983 CIC 1108 & 1085) that they would probably qualify for what canon law calls a "documentary process," that is, a process which can result in an annulment, but without the necessity of the full tribunal trial (1983 CIC 1686). Here, though, is where the mistake can occur.

Recognizing the vacuity of the first attempt at marriage, one might be tempted to treat it as a "marriage that didn't count" and simply not report it to the minister or tribunal. Maybe this information is withheld out of embarrassment, or to save time, or to spare the new intended spouse of ever knowing of the potentially painful past. But these are not reasons for non-disclosure, they are excuses, and they can be a recipe for disaster. How?

First, not every "open and shut" case qualifies for the quicker documentary procedure. Only the tribunal can make that determination. Second, not every nullity case, whether documentary or formal, results in a declaration of nullity. Again, only a Church court can make that determination.

Third, every relationship, including an invalid marriage, leaves its mark on a person. Sometimes, moreover, the factors which lead to an earlier invalid attempt at marriage might still be at work in a person. These factors should, maybe even must, be addressed before potentially repeating the same kinds of mistakes. This growth process, however, cannot even be initiated if the past remains hidden.

For these and other reasons, canon law forbids a "second" marriage before the invalidity of the "first" is officially established (1983 CIC 1085). Please note that, strictly speaking, canon 1085, if violated, does not doom the "second" marriage to invalidity. Nevertheless, persons considering marriage under these circumstances, or perhaps persons already married thereunder, should not hesitate to discuss the facts honestly with a priest or deacon and thereby receive advice on how to address these matters correctly.

Question 88:

Do some people get more than one annulment?

Although not typical, neither is it unheard of for someone to obtain more than one declaration of nullity. This could happen in a couple of ways. For example, a petitioner might present several serial marriages for adjudication all at once. Or, less often but more disturbingly, some years after getting an annulment in order to enter a second marriage, a petitioner might return seeking annulment of that second marriage, perhaps even in order to enter yet a third.

In any case, the reason for the multiplicity of annulments can be surprisingly simple: the factors which lead to the invalidity of marriage Number 1, if left unresolved, could still have been at work, and hence destroyed the validity of marriage Number 2, or Number 3, and so on. If this sounds to you like a vicious circle, all I can say is that it sounds that way to me, too. Unfortunately, when push comes to shove, canon law gives local Church authorities surprisingly little to prevent that scenario.

Question 89:

Are there too many annulments?

Y es, far too many. But let's be clear about what we
mean here. America's annulment picture—
whether in terms of raw numbers, percentage of
affirmatives decisions, or in comparison with the rest
of the world—is nothing to be proud of. If America
still functions administratively, it does so despite
Americans becoming increasingly dysfunctional (not
to overuse a term) personally. In declaring well over
50,000 marriages (not all of them Catholic, by the way)
null each year, America might be like the cancer-
stricken oncologist, smart enough to diagnose its own
matrimonial illnesses, but too weak to cure itself.

For cases involving a Catholic wedding, each
annulment represents another example of where
canon 1066—which calls the elimination of anything
which can affect the validity or liceity of a wedding
before the ceremony—was honored too late. Each
annulment, without doubt, represents a personal human tragedy, usually two human tragedies, and often
several human tragedies combined.

An annulment is sometimes presented as the first
step on the road to recovery in the life of Faith. Often
it is. But whatever else it might be, an annulment is
primarily proof of a defeat, perhaps self-inflicted or
socially pre-conditioned, but a failure nevertheless.

In answering yes to the question of whether there
are too many annulments, however, all one really does
is push the question back one step: what we need to
ask is not so much why are there so many annulments,
but instead why are there so many invalid marriages?

Question 90:

I know of a case in which the wife absolutely knocked herself out trying to save her marriage, and her husband, who was a real creep, got an annulment. How is that fair?

Some people sincerely, but very mistakenly, view marriage as something like a tennis doubles team in which the strengths of one player can compensate for the weaknesses of the other player to such a degree that the team, the marriage, wins in the end. But seldom in tennis, and strictly speaking never in marriage, do things work out that way.

Marriage, like doubles tennis, requires two people— not one, not one and one-half, nor even one and three-quarters, but two, complete, albeit fallen, people. Put me on a doubles court with a Wimbledon champ, and we'd get whipped by any pair of decent players. Why? Because Wimbledon champs can't play tennis? No, because *I* can't. The champ could complain all day long that he or she understood tennis, played well, deserved to be on a winning team, and so on. But the fact would remain, we lost.

Canon law is very clear: both spouses must be capable of and willing to enter marriage as the Church understands and proclaims it (1983 CIC 1057). The "super" capacity or commitment of one partner cannot be lent to the other, even though we all know that no two spouses are equal, let alone identical, in their total ability or willingness to make a marriage work. Moreover, that mutual capacity and consent must be present on the wedding day, for Church law does not allow for post-wedding maturation to supply retroactively for pre-wedding deficiencies.

Question 91:

I've been told that one of my two marriages is a "DF" case. What is a "DF"?

"DF" stands for "defect of canonical form." At the time of your DF wedding, either you, or your spouse, or both of you, were Catholic(s) bound by the requirements of canonical form (cf. 1983 CIC 1108 & 1117). Apparently, that form was not observed, or it was only incompletely observed, at the time of the wedding and hence that attempt at marriage must be declared null, probably by using an abbreviated tribunal procedure under canon 1686. While canonists technically distinguish between "lack of form" and "defect of form" cases, both types of cases, if proven, result in nullity as far as the spouses are concerned.

Don't make the mistake many people do, though, and assume that a DF case is not really an annulment. It most certainly is. The process for declaring nullity in such cases might be expedited and it might be less costly, but DF cases remain declarations of nullity. Indeed, roughly 25% of all the annulments declared each year in the United States are DF annulments. They contribute in a startling way, therefore, to the explosion of annulments in America.

Question 92:

I was born and raised Catholic, but I fell away from the Church while a young adult and joined an Evangelical Protestant church. During that time, I got married and later we divorced. I had a vague feeling that I should have gotten the Catholic Church's permission to marry, but because I was active in that other church, I let it slide. I've since come back to the Catholic Church, but I'm getting conflicting stories about my chances for an annulment. Some say that because I wasn't married in a Catholic ceremony, my marriage is automatically null, others have told me that the rules have changed and my former marriage might be valid. What's the story?

Your question boils down to whether or not you were bound by canonical form at the time of your wedding. If your wedding took place on or before November 26, 1983, that is, before the 1983 Code took effect, you were almost certainly bound by canonical form and, having evidently not observed it, your attempt at marriage was probably null under Church law.

But if your wedding took place on or after November 27, 1983, there's a good chance you were not bound by canonical form, in light of a new canon which exempts from the obligation of form those Catholics "who have left the Church by a formal act" (1983 CIC 1117). While the code does not define "formal act of defection," it's certainly speaking of something more than just "falling away" from the Faith, as you admit to doing. Joining a Protestant denomination and actively participating in it, on the other hand, will probably be held to qualify as a formal act of defection. If so, you would not have been bound to observe Catholic form at the time of your wedding, and your failure to have done so will not automatically result in the canonical nullity of your marriage.

Only a diocesan tribunal can render a judgment on the above scenarios, and you should certainly present the information as accurately as possible to the tribunal in order for it to arrive at a reliable conclusion on the issues. Don't make the mistake of considering this a "marriage that didn't count" and simply forgetting about it. If it turns out that you were not bound by form and hence that you cannot use that as the basis of impugning your marriage, you (or your former spouse, for that matter) would still be allowed to raise issues concerning matrimonial capacity and consent as possible bases for nullity. Again, though, only a diocesan tribunal can adjudicate those issues for you.

Question 93:

When I went into my first marriage, I did so with serious doubts that I was doing to right thing. I knew my ex-husband had been married before and that there was no annulment of that marriage. I went ahead with the wedding, though, because I figured that if things didn't work out, we could get divorced and I could apply for an annulment because of my ex's former marriage. I realize this sounds rather calculating, but was my thinking about the annulment correct?

If you are looking for a simple, albeit grudging, yes, I can't give you one. Canon law, and the Church it serves, has been around a long time. Schemes like yours are not new, and the Code has provisions which apply in cases like this.

First, the impediment of ligamen, or prior marriage bond, which you are counting on to deprive your former spouse of matrimonial capacity (1983 CIC 1085) only arises from a valid marriage. Now, while the Church generally presumes the validity of marriages that more or less look like marriages, it retains the authority to investigate virtually any marriage, including those whose validity directly affects the possible validity of a later marriage. If the tribunal from which you are seeking the annulment of your marriage doubts the validity of your ex-spouse's first marriage (and the Defender of the Bond and/or the Promoter of Justice are just the types to raise such questions if they choose), you could well end up with the tribunal being unable to reach moral certitude about the validity of your ex's first marriage, and hence being unable to reach moral certitude about his being bound by ligamen.

So, you try your second theory of nullity which runs thus: even if my ex-spouse wasn't validly married, I thought he was, and so when I consented to marriage, I didn't think it would be a valid marriage, and therefore I consented invalidly (1983 CIC 1057 § 2). Maybe, maybe not.

Little canon 1100, which is hiding way back in the provisions on consent, says that the knowledge or opinion of the nullity of a marriage does not necessarily prevent matrimonial consent from being given (cf. also 1983 CIC 1107). In other words, the mere fact (assuming it can be proven) that you reasonably felt your marriage would be invalid does not necessarily mean that the consent you (rather connivingly?) gave to that marriage is invalid. It might have been, and you'd be allowed to try to prove it. But it's not the canonical cake walk you, and others before you, have predicted. You would have to prove, among other things, that, but for your opinion of nullity, you would not have given your consent at all to your marriage. Perhaps you can prove this; but your already being engaged at the time you came up with this idea is going to give the Defender of the Bond some basis for challenging your claims on this point.

Now don't misunderstand. You have the same rights as anyone else to impugn your marriage, and even though your particular theories of nullity might not pan out as you hoped, you have, whether you know it or not, given other signs of possible nullity in your marriage. The point is merely this: be honest and accurate in your depiction of events, and let the tribunal determine whether you have presented a recognizable basis for nullity and, if so, whether you have produced sufficient evidence to prove your claim. Don't try to outwit the tribunal.

Question 94:

Will the tribunal speed up an annulment case because a pregnant woman needs it in order to get remarried in the Church?

No way. That simply sows the seeds of doubt about the woman's discretion of judgment (1983 CIC 1095, n.2) or submission to reverential fear (1983 CIC 1103) in entering a second marriage.

It has taken awhile, but we're finally getting to the point where social pressures to wed in response to a pre-marital pregnancy are fading. The last thing most diocesan tribunals want to do is encourage more such frequently short-sighted decisions. Even though pre-marital pregnancy is not grounds for an annulment, and even though, strictly speaking, a tribunal could take a case like the one you are describing out of turn, the chances of its doing so, and the prudence of its doing so, are very slim.

Question 95:

Prior to our civil marriage, my wife and I had both been married and divorced. We stopped receiving the sacraments after we got married to each other, although we still went to Mass. Since then, we both applied for annulments of our earlier marriages. My wife's annulment has already come through and I am told that mine will shortly. We plan to have our marriage blessed in the Church as soon as we can after that. Is our getting the annulments and having our marriage blessed all we need to do in order to be readmitted to the sacraments?

Whatever might have been the factors which lead you and your present spouse to marry outside of the Church, it's clear that you take the rest of the Church's sacramental life seriously and that you are sincerely trying to rectify your matrimonial status in the Church. Assuming things go as you have told, I would think the following.

Your annulment, and your spouse's, mean that the Church considers you to be single people free to marry each other. While it's often impractical for civilly married, but canonically single, people such as yourselves to separate (for example, there might be small children to care for) you should not, precisely as single people, make use of marital privileges (specifically, sexual intercourse).

The "blessing of your marriage," known technically as a "convalidation" (1983 CIC 1156–1160), would mean that the Church would consider you to be a married couple. From that point on, of course, there would be no moral bar to the exercise of marital rights, nor any canonical bar to sacramental participation based on your marital status.

But here is what I would invite you to think about: for a period of time in the past, you and your spouse were consciously in an invalid marriage, "living in sin," as some put it. While your annulment and convalidation puts an end to that irregular situation, it does not erase it. Christ does that, usually in confession. Canon 1065 § 2 strongly recommends that all those who are about to be married go to confession and receive Holy Eucharist beforehand. You and your spouse seem especially receptive to these opportunities for grace and growth, and I encourage you to talk with a spiritual director or confessor about what is best in your situation.

Question 96:

Before getting married, my ex-husband and I entered into a pre-nuptial contract in which we agreed, in the event of a divorce, not to contest each other's request for an annulment. Now he has broken that agreement and is fighting my nullity petition. What should I expect the diocesan tribunal to do about that?

Nothing. Such contracts have absolutely no force under canon law. Indeed, I can't imagine a Catholic minister officiating at a wedding if he knew that such a promise on future annulments had been made (1983 CIC 1066).

Ironically perhaps, the fact such a contract was even made raises, in my mind, certain questions about the sufficiency of the consent you exchanged at your wedding (cf., for example, 1983 CIC 1101 § 2 & 1102 § 1), but it will be for the tribunal to assess that matter in much more detail than is possible here. The mere fact that such a contract was made, I should say, would not automatically invalidate the marriage, although the tribunal will want to know about it and will want to consider what it might portend concerning the parties' attitude toward, for example, the permanence of marriage.

Question 97:

I have real problems with the Church's claim to be able to annul marriages. I don't see that in the Bible anywhere. What I do see is: "What God has joined, let no man put asunder." Please comment.

Generally, I let pass imprecisions in questions be cause such imprecisions don't usually affect the answer. But here, they might. The Church does not claim the power to annul marriages if by that you mean the power to transform something that was into something that isn't. An annulment case, assuming it "goes affirmative," is the Church declaring, or recognizing, that what seemed, perhaps very reasonably, to have been a valid marriage, was not one. I understand that this is a distinction which is hard for some people to make, and which a generally cynical age dismisses as hocus-pocus. Well, and no disrespect intended, that's their problem. In the meantime, it's simply wrong to attribute to the Church a power which even it denies it has (1983 CIC 1141).

There are lots of instances in which the Church is called upon to defend—if only in the court of public opinion—powers that it uses. That's fine. But in the case of annulments, no specific power is being used against a marriage. To the contrary, as is true for every advanced society, the Church has a mechanism for investigating the actual binding nature of the commitments apparently made among its members. These investigations do not negate the power of people to commit themselves to a certain status; rather these procedures are used to determine whether that power was in fact employed in a specific instance.

That said, there are few (very few) types of valid marriages which can be dissolved (not annulled) under certain circumstances. Marriages which were never consummated, for example, represent one kind of case in which dissolution might be possible (1983 CIC 1142). Likewise, marriages of the unbaptized could, I repeat could, under certain circumstances, be dissolved by a second marriage (not by the Church) if it serves the Christian life of the newly baptized spouse (cf. 1983 CIC 1143–1147). Note, though, that in these latter cases, the source of the practice is not so much canon law, but St. Paul's teaching in I Corinthians 7:12–15.

Question 98:

I understand that I need an annulment before I can enter the Church, but I have been told that the backlog of cases is two years, sometimes three. Why should I be kept waiting that long?

No one is happy with tribunal backlogs, and they can work a real hardship on people. Despite canons which encourage nullity cases to be processed (not necessarily granted) with one and one half years (cf. 1983 CIC 1453) backlogs of cases beyond those time limits do exist. There are a couple of options which might be tried.

If the case is a very solid one with excellent supporting testimony, you or your advocate could ask that it be taken out of turn, especially if resolution of the case is necessary for entrance into the Church or convalidation of an otherwise apparently stable family relationship (1983 CIC 1458). Understand that many petitions might meet that standard, though, and that the tribunal need not grant it. Alternatively, it is possible that other tribunals, if they are equally competent to hear the case, could be approached to accept the case under certain circumstances.

In any case, do not try to come into the Church until your marital status is settled, even if a well-intentioned pastor is willing to accept you because "it's not your fault that your open-and-shut nullity case can't be heard for some time." Not all open-and-shut cases really are open-and-shut, and there is also the chance that certain restrictions on a future marriage might be imposed by the tribunal. Besides, as long as one is in an irregular union, one simply is not eligible for full sacramental participation (1983 CIC 205 & 915). Having seen, correctly, the value of Church membership, don't let it be cheapened by coming in irregularly.

Question 99:

You quoted canon law a lot in your answers. Can lay people have copies of canon law?

Certainly. Useful English versions of current canon law include the following: *Code of Canon Law/Latin-English Edition*, published by the Canon Law Society of America; and *The Code of Canon Law in English Translation*, published by William B. Eerdmans. Each of these are available from, or at least can be ordered through, local Catholic bookstores.

Question 100:

Our neighbors were divorced a few years back, and recently the marriage was annulled because the wife was pregnant at the time of their wedding. This has greatly upset me because I was pregnant when I got married, too, but I feel perfectly fine in my marriage. Am I living in a null marriage?

Your marriage is presumptively valid (1983 CIC 1060), but your question illustrates well the dangers of incomplete, even erroneous, understandings about how the annulment process works. Your neighbor's marriage was not annulled because she was pregnant at the time of the wedding. It couldn't have been. Pregnancy at the time of marriage is not grounds for an annulment. Your neighbor's marriage was annulled because, and only because, the tribunal system found with moral certainty that one or both of the parties to that marriage suffered from invalidating flaws in matrimonial capacity, consent, or form. If pregnancy was relevant to the nullity petition, and it often is, it's only because that condition shed light on other serious problems dooming the marriage before it ever started.

My wife went to the dentist last week. When she came back, she told me the dentist had found a cavity. Now, we eat the same foods, we observe the same dental hygiene, we're the same age, etc., and I'm going to the same dentist next week. My wife's experience does not doom me to having a cavity, does it? People should never try to analyze their marriage situation based on the experiences of similarly situated family or friends. If someone has a question about the canonical status of their marriage, especially if the marriage is intact, they may do as you did, and seek qualified advice. But in any event, they should, as the Church does, presume the validity of their marriage.

XII. Annulments in America: Keeping Bad News in Context

Thoughtful Americans are disturbed at the high number of divorces in the United States. But some observers look at the concomitantly sharp rise in declarations of matrimonial nullity (commonly called annulments) being granted by American diocesan tribunals and suggest, if not conclude, that U.S. tribunals are capitulating to the divorce mentality, perhaps even fanning its flames.

The criticisms made against American tribunals spring from a wide variety of sources and take a wide variety of forms. Too numerous to cite here, these sources of criticism include Vatican officials, heterodox and orthodox clerics and laity, and virtually all major organs of Catholic opinion. The criticisms offered by these disparate sources include: annulments are being granted too quickly, they are not being granted quickly enough, tribunals overuse the consent canons as a basis for nullity, they are only scratching the surface of the consent canons in nullity cases, annulments are only for the rich, annulments are wasting diocesan resources, and so on. Serving, however, as the fire which keeps this hot pot of debate boiling is the tremendous surge in American annulment activity. In most fields, of course, raw numbers and their ratios are only used as measures of institutional activity. But in the annulment context, tribunal statistics themselves are often used, consciously or otherwise, as actual criticisms of tribunal activity. These criticisms are posed by means of what I call the "numbers stick."

The statistically-oriented "numbers stick" generally takes one of three forms: 1) the great rise in the total number of American annulments means that there is something wrong with U.S. tribunals; 2) the relatively high ratio of affirmative decisions granted in America means that there is something wrong with U.S. tribunals; and 3) the generally disproportionate tribunal activity in America means that there is something wrong with U.S. tribunals. This article will examine the "numbers stick" to see how it fares under rebuttal.

I

In the early 1960s, about 300 declarations of nullity came from the United States each year; today that annual figure has grown to over 60,000.[1] By any measure, that is a staggering increase. But is this huge increase in annulments a sign of tribunal laxity toward marriage or complicity in its demise?

Consider: during the same decades in which declarations of matrimonial nullity were soaring in the

U.S., similarly huge increases in, for example, product liability awards and successful prosecutions for child abuse were experienced in the civil arena. Are these phenomena, however, taken as proof of dysfunction in the American legal system? Not usually. Rather, they are the direct result of major changes made in the underlying civil laws governing such cases, changes which not only made some kinds of jury awards and criminal convictions more likely, but which in turn encouraged more cases to be filed under the revised laws.[2] Similarly, some very significant changes in canonical procedure have been made over the last 30 years, changes which facilitated both the filing of marriage nullity petitions and the chances that such petitions will be proven. But these changes, being technical in nature, tended to pass unnoticed by the average tribunal observer.

To take just one example, up until 1969, canon law basically allowed annulment petitions to be filed only in the diocese wherein the wedding was celebrated or in the diocese wherein the respondent (the other party to the marriage) currently lived. But beginning in 1970, the Holy See approved for use in the United States a modified canonical procedure which allowed petitioners to file their nullity cases in the diocese in which they currently lived, regardless of where the wedding was celebrated or where their ex-spouse now lived.[3] The implications of this one canonical change in a country like America were enormous.

Recall that, not only are Americans generally prone to be mobile over the years, but marital failure accelerates and compounds that predilection in that divorcees are even more apt to change their surroundings as part of starting a new life. Since 1970, how-

ever, no longer were divorced Catholics required by
canon law to return to the place of the wedding or
the territory of their former spouse in order to have
their petition for nullity heard. The petitioner, always
a motivated and knowledgeable party, can now have
his petition heard in the tribunal most convenient to
himself.[4]

Tribunal competence was just one area in which
canonical procedures were significantly revised by
Rome in ways that facilitated matrimonial nullity fil-
ings and declarations. Other procedural changes included allowing a single judge to hear a case instead
of requiring three judges to hear each petition, and
eliminating caps on the number of qualified judges
allowed to serve in a diocese; eliminating restrictions
which prevented "guilty" spouses from seeking annulments, and allowing non-Catholics to file cases in
diocesan tribunals; eliminating several of the more
archaic regulations on the types of evidence allowed
and the numbers of witnesses needed in nullity cases;
and imposing new, or shortening old, time limits for
the speedier treatment of marriage cases. Each of
these Roman changes in procedural canon law have
indisputably contributed to the dramatic increase in
declarations of marriage nullity.[5]

As important as were the procedural changes
above, they combined in potent fashion with the
Roman decision to include in the 1983 Code a single
new norm on marriage consent, namely canon 1095.
Of the 15 or 20 possible grounds upon which a
marriage case can be heard (1983 CIC 1083–1105),
more nullity petitions are adjudged on the basis of
canon 1095 than on all the others combined.[6] Canon
1095 of the revised Code, without precedent in the
old Code, is the single canon which most directly

allows tribunals to address the canonical impact of mental, emotional, personal, psychological, psychiatric, and even chemical traumas suffered by persons attempting marriage.

Like most first attempts at legislating on complex areas, canon 1095 suffers, I think, from certain conceptual problems and has been subject to various schools of interpretation whose analysis is beyond the scope of this article which I have limited to the statistically-oriented complaints against U.S. tribunals. But the fundamental insight of canon 1095 is crucial in helping the Church confront accurately the modern crises in marriage: canon 1095, for all its flaws, is still the best tool for addressing cases in which drug and alcohol abuse, physical or sexual abuse, psychological and psychiatric anomalies, and a variety of other mental and emotional conditions have seriously impacted parties prior to marriage.

Frankly, to attack American tribunals on the basis that, under canon 1095, they are declaring null tens of thousands more marriages than they did a few decades ago is akin to attacking American hospitals on the basis that they are diagnosing tens of thousands more cases of HIV/AIDS than they did a few decades ago. That analogy might be unfair in that HIV/AIDS apparently did not exist 30 years ago, whereas fallen human nature and divorce did. Nevertheless, no credible social observer takes the position that average levels of personal maturity or individual integrity—two very important factors in canon 1095 cases—have done anything but plummet over the last 30 years.

Consider: Most tribunal critics recognize well the profound truth of the Church teachings contained in *Humanae Vitae*. Yet I see no acknowledgment by tribunal critics that the wholesale disregard for, or ignorance of, those teachings among lay Catholics (to say nothing of non-Catholics coming before diocesan tribunals) is having any significant impact on the attempts of such people to enter marriage. The use of contraceptives, even abortifacients, is not a canonical impediment to marriage (this comes as a surprise to many tribunal critics) but, whether as cause or effect, it seems highly correlative of the startling, and ultimately destructive, levels of immaturity and irresponsibility which so many people try to bring to marriage today. For that matter, stories of heterodox, including pro-contraceptive, ecclesiastical marriage preparation programs and sex education classes are legion. Cannot such programs (some of them in place for over 20 years now) be having exactly the kind of grave anti-family/anti-marriage effects that opponents rightly fear?

Before leaving the topic of the huge increase in the basic number of annulments declared in the U.S., one final but very important point should be considered: namely, the affect of canonical form requirements on annulment numbers. This requirement of canonical form is what causes "Las Vegas style" weddings to be invalid for Catholics; indeed, such weddings are so obviously canonically invalid that they qualify for a faster documentary process for declaring such marriages null.[7] But, second only to annulments based on canon 1095, more U.S. annulments are based on violations of canonical form than on any other cause. In 1991, for example, nearly 18,700 of the 63,900 American declarations of nullity were based on violations of canonical form.[8]

Tribunal judges have virtually no discretion in the handling of canonical form cases; it is as close to an utterly objective type of case as canon law has.[9] And yet canonical form cases consistently account for up to 25% of all the annulments being granted in America.[10] Even if, therefore, one were to argue that American tribunals consistently misinterpret the psychological canons on consent, one is still left having to account for the huge number of canonical form nullity cases, which numbers, standing alone, still dwarf the total number of pre-APN annulments declared in the U.S.

II

The second category of "numbers stick" criticism concedes the irrelevance of the increase in raw numbers of annulments, but argues that the ratio of affirmative decisions to petitions is so high as to support a suspicion of pervasive "anti-marriage/pro-nullity" biases on the part of most tribunal judges. The criticism is commonly put: American tribunals nullify 95% of the marriages that come before them.

The first time I heard this criticism, I conceded, pro arguendo, the accuracy of the percentage (something I would not do today, for the reasons discussed below.) But I then asked the critic whether he considered American municipal courts generally fair in their treatment of the cases which come before them. We both agreed that such courts are generally considered fair and effective, at which point I observed that the conviction rate of defendants in such courts usually exceeds 90%. While no one wants to equate traffic tickets with broken families, the comparison does suggest a danger in forming conclusions about the fairness of courts, or tribunals, based solely on the way the majority of cases are decided in such fora.[11]

Today, however, I would dispute the percentage of annulments which some claim are being granted. But to understand this rebuttal one must have a basic grasp of the major stages in processing a marriage case.

Virtually every nullity petition which ends up in an affirmative tribunal decision begins as an interview in a pastor's office. This is a practically useful, but technically unofficial, part of most tribunals' procedures, and hence is not given to close monitoring. And yet, while most pastors (or their staffs) are very willing to assist potential petitioners in drafting their forms for the tribunal, it also happens that, based on discussions with pastors or staff, some potential petitioners are dissuaded from filing their petitions, usually because the pastor has stated, or even just hinted at, his opinion that the case "probably won't be approved by the tribunal." My hunch (and that is all I have on this point) is that those pastors are usually right. The petition probably would have been a weak one, and it probably would not have been approved in a formal trial.

Assuming completion of the parish-based paperwork, potential petitions are forwarded to the diocesan tribunal. In a preliminary procedure, those potential petitions are examined for routine things like the presence of necessary supporting documents such as baptismal and wedding certificates, divorce decrees, etc. Here again, though, the opportunity arises, this time for tribunal personnel, to suggest either to the pastor or directly to the potential petitioner withdrawing the potential petition because of what appear to be factors which typically prevent an affirmative decision. Being the recommendation of canonical experts, such informal suggestions are even more likely to be on point, resulting in again more weak cases being eliminated before officially entering the tribunal system.

Even after official acceptance of a petition, however, it can happen that a petitioner loses interest in the case, or witnesses fail to come forward in a useful manner, or other factors emerge which prevent the case from moving forward. Almost invariably, a petition which "stalls" does so for the same types of reasons which would have resulted, had the case gone to sentence, in its being denied. With these major, if not always official, stages in mind, let's examine some of the statistics on apparent affirmative rates in U.S. tribunals.

In 1991 some 48,600 petitions were considered as presented to American tribunals.[12] Of those, only 43,900 were accepted for adjudication and, of those, only about 39,100 were decided by formal sentences. Assume that almost all of these sentences were affirmative. That is still only an 89% affirmative rate among cases actually accepted, and barely 80% for those cases officially presented. Moreover, the affirmative rate drops even more when one recalls that additional weak cases are weeded out at the parish level or perhaps presented only in part to the tribunal and some cases go negative.

One could, I suppose, maintain that even this 80% affirmative rate is too high—although how one could do that without examining individual cases escapes me. What response then? Well, it might be worth comparing the U.S. affirmative rate with Rome's, specifically the Roman Rota's.

According to Augustine Mendonca's recently published Rotal Anthology, during, for example, the three years surrounding the promulgation of the revised Code of Canon Law, 1982 through 1984, the Roman Rota heard 571 cases dealing with matrimonial nullity, and reached an affirmative result in 354 of them, for a 62% affirmative rate.[13] Certainly no one I know accuses the Roman Rota of being soft on marriage cases. While Rome's apparent 62% affirmative rate is not as high as America's apparent 80% rate, neither is it as low as some might think.

Of course, any number of factors might have influenced the Rota's affirmative percentage—things like taking cases from around the world, or like its serving extensively as an appellate court—and such factors should be considered in assessing the Rota's performance. But cannot procedural or demographic factors affect American tribunal performance, too? In any event, some recognition that over half of the marriage cases handled by the Roman Rota apparently end in an affirmative sentence seems in order.[14]

Finally, to the degree that percentages are relevant at all, one might query what percentage of divorced Catholics in America have actually received a declaration of nullity. Speculation on this point is hampered because there do not appear to be firm figures on just how many divorced (albeit perhaps remarried) Catholics there are in America.[15] But reasonable estimates on the percentage of divorced Catholics in America who have received a declaration of nullity range anywhere from 5% to 25%. I'll go with 10% and ask: is that ratio really too high?

Should we not expect the Church's teaching on marriage, which is reflected in its canon law, to shed some light on the causes of modern matrimonial collapse? In every ten failed Catholic marriages, should we be surprised that at least one of those marriages failed for the very reasons which Church law itself tried to warn would result in invalidity?

Or are we to hold that the canon law on marriage—and the Church teaching it upholds—is so irrelevant to modern married life that its disregard by couples will have no actual impact on their lives and marriages in this world? Or, on the other hand, does a couple's demonstrable respect for the Church's marriage requirements offer no protection against the ravages of divorce? Ideally, of course, there ought to be no divorces and no annulments, but if there are to be civil divorces, canonical nullity should account for a significant percentage of those failed marriages.[16]

III

The third category of "numbers stick" criticism prescinds from the first two critiques outlined above, and focuses on the indisputably anomalous situation of American tribunals as compared to the rest of the world. This critique is often put: American Catholics make up 5% of the world's Catholic population, but they get 80% of the Catholic world's annulments.[17]

I frankly feel that this is the shallowest of all tribunal criticisms. Americans make up 6% of the world's population, but they account for 100% of the men on the moon. So what? America functions. Much of the rest of the world does not.

American tribunals keep sufficient and reliable office hours, their telephones work, their mail is delivered on time, and if their photocopy machine breaks down, replacement parts are not six months away. Most of the parties and witnesses in an American nullity case will be able to drive to the tribunal in their own car on a paved road without hinderance by anything from fuel shortages to partisans in civil wars. In an almost incalculable and invisible number of ways, American Catholics have the leisure, in the classical sense of the word, to worry about their juridic status in the Church. Do we really expect a plethora of nullity cases to be processed from Catholics in communist China, Bosnia, or some third-world drug republic?

Well, one might rejoin, what about those countries where a Hobbesian hell does not hold sway? For the most part, such countries are either industrialized Pacific rim nations like Japan, with virtually no Catholic population, or they are a western European country like France or the Netherlands with what, in comparison to the U.S., can fairly be called a notably apathetic Catholic population.

Ever since De Tocqueville penned his classic study of America, historians have recognized that the average American takes religious issues much more seriously than does the average European, and, moreover, that Americans are markedly more concerned about legal procedures, rights and duties. What people of what nation, therefore, would be more inclined by desire and more able in means than Americans to use a religio-legal procedure like annulments to assess their canonical status in their Church?

Of course, if one still wishes to criticize America for its disproportional tribunal activity, one could just as easily, and just as misleadingly, point out that Italy, with just 5% of the world's Catholic population, accounts for at least 70% of the Roman Rota's case load; indeed, the Rota grants more annulments to Italians than it does to the rest of the world combined.[18] But if one cannot take those patently disproportionate Italian figures and conclude that Rome is winking at marriage (even at Italian marriage), why should one be allowed to take America's similarly disproportionate annulment statistics and conclude that U.S. tribunals are lax in their administration of canonical justice?

I do not wish to be misunderstood: America's annulment picture, whether in terms of its raw numbers, its percentage of affirmatives decisions, or in comparison with the rest of the world, is nothing to be proud of. Like a cancer-stricken oncologist, America might be smart enough to diagnose its own illnesses, but unable to cure itself.

Each annulment represents, without any hyperbole, a personal human tragedy, usually two human tragedies, and often several human tragedies combined. And, for those cases which involved a Catholic wedding, each annulment represents yet another example of where canon 1066—which calls the elimination of anything which can affect the validity or liceity of a wedding before the ceremony—was honored too late.[19]

The news on American annulments is bad, but that bad news should be kept in context. Most certainly, I do not take the position that American tribunals are above reproach in their handling of nullity cases, and some of the substantive, as opposed to statistical, criticisms of American tribunal practice do deserve closer attention. But I am sure I'm not alone among tribunal personnel when I feel that modern American tribunals are still being held accountable for some of the rash statements made by some American canonists during the first heady days of American Procedural Norms. In any event, it serves no purpose to attack today's tribunals for, I think, accurately "diagnosing" the extent of the divorce disease among Americans.

Certainly, I have opinions on how we might come to grips with the on-going collapse of the American, and Catholic, family. Other people have theirs. Most of all, though, the Church has its grace and wisdom to apply. So, if this study only helps eliminate the less fruitful ideas for reform, especially the idea that there's nothing wrong with Catholic American marriages that can't be fixed by shutting down American diocesan tribunals, I shall be satisfied.

This is a slightly modified version of an article which first appeared in the November 1996 issue of *Homiletic and Pastoral Review*.

Notes

1. See *The Code of Canon Law: A Text and Commentary*, (Paulist: New York, 1985), hereafter CLSA Commentary, at p. 1010, and *1994 Catholic Almanac* (Huntington: Our Sunday Visitor), 236, reporting for the year 1991. Throughout this article, 1991 is chosen as a typical year because its data is widely available, but it falls several years after the promulgation of the 1983 Code of Canon Law, meaning that virtually all nullity cases heard now are being treated in light of the new law.

2. Some changes in American law are the result of judicial attitudes being substituted, rightly or wrongly, for legislative intent. But in canon law,

such a feat is virtually impossible. The Code of Canon Law is replete with effective restrictions on the ability of anyone beside the legislator to change substantive or procedural law (see, eg., 1983 CIC 8, 16, 17, 19, 1404–1406 & 1417). Not even the Roman Rota can interpret canon law contrary to the Pope's intentions.

3. Cf. "Provisional Norms for Marriage Annulment Cases in [the] United States," 28 April 1970, *Canon Law Digest,* VII 950–966. The "American Procedural Norms" had been drafted by the Canon Law Society of America in the mid to late 1960s and proposed for Roman approval by the National Conference of Catholic Bishops shortly later. Absent Roman authorization, the APN would have remained speculative exercises by academics; but after Roman approval, they became binding law in U.S. tribunals. Afterward, if an American tribunal judge, fearful that these new procedural norms would threaten the stability of marriage, had refused to accept a petition correctly filed under the APN, canon law itself would have threatened him with sanctions up to and including removal from office. See 1917 CIC 1625 § 1 and 1983 CIC 1457. Many of the more "liberalizing" provisions of the APN were later made applicable throughout the Roman Catholic world as part of Pope Paul VI's apostolic letter *Causas matrimoniales,* 28 March 1971, *Canon Law Digest,* VII 969–974, AAS 63–441.

4. The current law, 1983 CIC 1673, n. 3, differs from the APN only in requiring the consent of the respondent's judicial vicar, who in turn need only hear (not obtain the consent of) the respondent. Most requests for competence filed under 1673, n. 3, are approved because: A) most respondents do

not in fact object to a "foreign" tribunal hearing their ex-spouse's petition; and B) the relatively few respondents who do object, usually object not to the hearing of the case in the diocese of their ex-spouse, but rather to any tribunal's hearing the case—something respondents clearly have no canonical right to assert.

5. The Holy See incorporated most of these APN-type provisions in the 1983 Code with full awareness of the impact such procedures were having on American nullity cases. The Canon Law Society of America had been reporting annually the explosion in American nullity cases regularly since the mid-1970s, and arguments against continuing the APN were raised by Roman dicasteries as early as 1973. See *Canon Law Digest,* VIII 1155–1157 & 1167–1169. Additional criticisms of the APN were raised by the Signatura in 1977 and in 1978, some five years before the 1983 Code took effect. See *Canon Law Digest,* IX 979–987 and *Canon Law Digest,* X 256–262. For a more recent Roman acknowledgement that the 1983 Code does increase the chances of proving invalid marriages null, see the appendix for the Congregation for the Doctrine of the Faith's Letter on "Reception of Communion: Divorced-and-Remarried Catholics," 14 September 1994, Para. 9, which states in part "The discipline of the Church, while it confirms the exclusive competence of ecclesiastical tribunals with respect to the examination of the validity of the marriage of Catholics, also offers new ways to demonstrate the nullity of a previous marriage in order to exclude as far as possible every divergence between the truth verifiable in the judicial process and the objective truth known

by a correct conscience." More recently still, *Newsweek* reported (5 February 1996, p. 6) that the Pope has urged the Roman Rota "to get moving on its backlog of annulment requests."

6. This is not entirely due to the very broad scope of canon 1095. It is also because many of the grounds for nullity address fact situations which are very rarely encountered in America. We have, for example, hardly any 15 year old boys attempting church weddings (c. 1083) and very few kidnapped woman being forced to marry their captors (c. 1089). Likewise, "AWOL" priests and religious rarely come back and seek annulments of their marriages (cc. 1087 & 1088).

7. See generally 1983 CIC 1108, 1127 & 1686–1688.

8. Cf. *1994 Catholic Almanac*, 236.

9. One could also consider so-called "ligamen" petitions, that is, cases in which nullity must be declared because at least one of the parties was shown already to be in a presumably valid marriage (1983 CIC 1085 § 1, eligible for expedited hearing under 1983 CIC 1686). In 1991, for example, over 2,200 American annulments were granted on the basis of ligamen, or prior bond, on the part of one or both parties to the impugned marriage. See "Tribunal Statistics Summary," *CLSA Proceedings* (1992), 252–268. Ironically, these annulments based on ligamen provided over 2,200 more times one could attack American tribunals for disregarding the sanctity of marriage, when in fact they were literally upholding it.

10. Rome might be reconsidering the automatic nullity implications of canonical form attendant to Catholic baptism. Canon 1117 now exempts from the requirement of canonical form Catholics "who

have left the Church by a formal act." Presumably, somewhat fewer marriages involving Catholics can be declared null solely on the basis of lack of canonical form. But see appendix one for the Congregation for the Doctrine of the Faith's, Letter on "Reception of Communion: Divorced-and-Remarried Catholics," 14 September 1994, Para. 9, which states in part "Adherence to the Church's judgment and observance of the existing discipline concerning the obligation of canonical form necessary for the validity of the marriage of Catholics are what truly contribute to the spiritual welfare of the faithful concerned."

11. The population treated in diocesan tribunals and municipal courts is obviously relevant to, though not dispositive of, their conclusions on particular cases. Take the first hundred drivers passing in front of one's house, and the first hundred drivers sitting in traffic court, and ask which group is more likely to contain a higher number of offenders. Likewise, take the first hundred families at a mall, and the first hundred arguing sets of spouses in divorce court (a civil divorce is a virtual prerequisite to filing a canonical petition for nullity), and ask which group is more likely to have more people in invalid marriages.

12. See "Tribunal Statistics Summary," *CLSA Proceedings* (1992), 252–268.

13. See A. Mendonca, *Rotal Anthology: An Annotated Index of Rotal Decisions from 1971 to 1988,* (Washington, DC: Canon Law Society of America, 1992), 755–769.

14. For the entire period 1971–1988, Mendonca lists 236 Rotal cases as coming from America, 127 (52%) of which went affirmative. See Mendonca,

Rotal Anthology, 688–695. If, however, a tribunal critic were to try to take this lower figure and argue that only 50% of American annulment petitions would, after Rotal review, be considered as proven (for many reasons, this would be a difficult argument to make) that would still suggest that well over 30,000 U.S. declarations of nullity would be provable each year. While that lower figure is roughly half the current U.S. annual formal nullity total, it remains over 100 times higher than the pre-APN numbers in America.

15. The *1994 Catholic Almanac*, 235, suggests that at least 6 million American Catholics have been divorced at least one time. Lawrence Wrenn estimated that, in the late 1970s, only one-half of one percent of all divorced Catholics in America were receiving annulments each year. *CLSA Commentary*, page 1010. V. Pospishil, "Response to Role of Law Award," *CLSA Proceedings* (1994) 270–273, at 272, suggests that over 160,000 Catholic couples (out of 1.1 million American divorces) split up each year, but that only 10% of those couples will ever file a nullity petition.

16. There is a third possibility: namely, that tens of thousands, perhaps hundreds of thousands, of American Catholics bring completely sufficient marriage skills to the altar, but then disregard natural and ecclesiastical law in divorcing each other and (usually) remarrying outside of the Church, only to then turn around and seek an ecclesiastical annulment of their first marriage for reasons unrelated, and sometimes even antithetical, to the conjugal truth of their situation. Such a perverse exercise of the free will, on such a massive scale, is, as a matter of moral theology,

possible. Whether this is a plausible explanation of the American annulment avalanche, I think, remains to be seen.

17. The statistics are basically correct. According to the *1994 Catholic Almanac*, 59,220,000 American Catholics make up 6.2% of the world's 949,578,000 Catholic population. In 1991, the U.S. accounted for 63,900 (79%) of the world's 80,700 annulments.

18. Mendonca, *Rotal Anthology*, pp. 590–698, takes 108 pages to list, by country of origin, all Rotal marriage cases from 1971–1988. Italy alone takes up 76 of those pages (compared to America's less than 7 pages), and a sampling of the Italian pages shows an affirmative rate of at least 50%.

19. Those pastors who do try to prevent a disaster-waiting-to-happen from getting married face numerous canonical obstacles to their efforts. See, for example, 1983 CIC 18, 213, 1058, and 1077. But see 1983 CIC 1071–1072.

Appendix 1

Letter to the Bishops of the Catholic Church Concerning the Reception of Holy Communion by Divorced and Remarried Members of the Faithful. Issued by the Sacred Congregation for the Doctrine of the Faith

1. The International Year of the Family is a particularly important occasion to discover anew the many signs of the Church's love and concern for the family[1] and, at the same time, to present once more the priceless riches of Christian marriage which is the basis of the family.

2. In this context the difficulties and sufferings of those faithful in irregular marriage situations merit special attention.[2] Pastors are called to help them experience the charity of Christ and the maternal closeness of the Church, receiving them with love, exhorting them to trust in God's mercy and suggesting, with prudence and respect, concrete ways of conversion and participation in the life of the community of the Church.[3]

3. Aware however that authentic understanding and genuine mercy are never separated from the truth,[4] pastors have the duty to remind these

faithful of the Church's doctrine concerning the celebration of the sacraments, in particular, the reception of the Holy Eucharist. In recent years, in various regions, different pastoral solutions in this area have been suggested according to which, to be sure, a general admission of the divorced and remarried to Eucharistic Communion would not be possible, but divorced and remarried members of the faithful could approach Holy Communion in specific cases when they consider themselves authorized according to a judgment of conscience to do so. This would be the case, for example, when they had been abandoned completely unjustly, although they sincerely tried to save the previous marriage, or when they are convinced of the nullity of their previous marriage, although unable to demonstrate it in the external forum or when they have gone through a long period of reflection and penance, or also when for morally valid reasons they cannot satisfy the obligation to separate.

In some places, it has also been proposed that in order objectively to examine their actual situation, the divorced and remarried would have to consult a prudent and expert priest. This priest, however, would have to respect their eventual decision in conscience to approach Holy Communion, without this implying an official authorization.

In these and similar cases it would be a matter of a tolerant and benevolent pastoral solution in order to do justice to the different situations of the divorced and remarried.

4. Even if analogous pastoral solutions have been proposed by a few fathers of the Church and in

some measure were practiced, nevertheless these never attained the consensus of the fathers and in no way came to constitute the common doctrine of the Church nor to determine her discipline. It falls to the universal magisterium, in fidelity to sacred Scripture and Tradition, to teach and to interpret authentically the *depositum fidei.*

With respect to the aforementioned new pastoral proposals, this congregation deems itself obliged therefore to recall the doctrine and discipline of the Church in this matter. In fidelity to the words of Jesus Christ,[5] the Church affirms that a new union cannot be recognized as valid if the preceding marriage was valid. If the divorced are remarried civilly, they find themselves in a situation that objectively contravenes God's law. Consequently, they cannot receive Holy Communion as long as this situation persists.[6]

This norm is not at all a punishment or a discrimination against the divorced and remarried, but rather expresses an objective situation that of itself renders impossible the reception of Holy Communion: "They are unable to be admitted thereto from the fact that their state and condition of life objectively contradict that union of love between Christ and his Church which is signified and effected by the Eucharist. Besides this, here is another special pastoral reason: If these people were admitted to the Eucharist, the faithful would be led into error and confusion regarding the Church's teaching about the indissolubility of marriage."[7]

The faithful who persist in such a situation may receive Holy Communion only after obtaining sacramental absolution, which may be given only "to those who, repenting of having broken the sign of the covenant and of fidelity to Christ, are sincerely ready to undertake a way of life that is no longer in contradiction to the indissolubility of marriage. This means, in practice, that when for serious reasons, for example, for the children's upbringing, a man and a woman cannot satisfy the obligation to separate, they 'take on themselves the duty to live in complete continence, that is, by abstinence from the acts proper to married couples.'"[8] In such a case they may receive Holy Communion as long as they respect the obligation to avoid giving scandal.

5. The doctrine and discipline of the Church in this matter are amply presented in the post-conciliar period in the apostolic exhortation *Familiaris Consortio*. The exhortation, among other things, reminds pastors that out of love for the truth they are obliged to discern carefully the different situations and exhorts them to encourage the participation of the divorced and remarried in the various events in the life of the Church. At the same time it confirms and indicates the reasons for the constant and universal practice, "founded on sacred Scripture, of not admitting the divorced and remarried to Holy Communion."[9] The structure of the exhortation and the tenor of its words give clearly to understand that this practice, which is presented as binding, cannot be modified because of different situations.

6. Members of the faithful who live together as husband and wife with persons other than their legitimate spouses may not receive Holy Communion. Should they judge it possible to do so, pastors and confessors, given the gravity of the

matter and the spiritual good of these persons,[10] as well as the common good of the Church, have the serious duty to admonish them that such a judgment of conscience openly contradicts the Church's teaching.[11] Pastors in their teaching must also remind the faithful entrusted to their care of this doctrine.

This does not mean that the Church does not take to heart the situation of these faithful, who moreover are not excluded from ecclesial communion. She is concerned to accompany them pastorally and invite them to share in the life of the Church in the measure that is compatible with the dispositions of divine law, from which the Church has no power to dispense.[12] On the other hand, it is necessary to instruct these faithful so that they do not think their participation in the life of the Church is reduced exclusively to the question of the reception of the Eucharist. The faithful are to be helped to deepen their understanding of the value of sharing in the sacrifice of Christ in the Mass, of spiritual communion,[13] of prayer, of meditation on the word of God, and of works of charity and justice.[14]

7. The mistaken conviction of a divorced and remarried person that he may receive Holy Communion normally presupposes that personal conscience is considered in the final analysis to be able, on the basis of one's own convictions,[15] to come to a decision about the existence or absence of a previous marriage and the value of the new union. However, such a position is inadmissible.[16] Marriage, in fact, both because it is the image of the spousal relationship between Christ and his Church as well as the fundamental core and an

important factor in the life of civil society, is essentially a public reality.

8. It is certainly true that a judgment about one's own dispositions for the reception of Holy Communion must be made by a properly formed moral conscience. But it is equally true that the consent that is the foundation of marriage is not simply a private decision since it creates a specifically ecclesial and social situation for the spouses, both individually and as a couple. Thus the judgment of conscience of one's own marital situation does not regard only the immediate relationship between man and God, as if one could prescind from the Church's mediation that also includes canonical laws binding in conscience. Not to recognize this essential aspect would mean in fact to deny that marriage is a reality of the Church, that is to say, a sacrament.

9. In inviting pastors to distinguish carefully the various situations of the divorced and remarried, the exhortation *Familiaris Consortio* recalls the case of those who are subjectively certain in conscience that their previous marriage, irreparably broken, had never been valid.[17] It must be discerned with certainty by means of the external forum established by the Church whether there is objectively such a nullity of marriage. The discipline of the Church, while it confirms the exclusive competence of ecclesiastical tribunals with respect to the examination of the validity of the marriage of Catholics, also offers new ways to demonstrate the nullity of a previous marriage, in order to exclude as far as possible every divergence between the truth verifiable in the judicial

process and the objective truth known by a correct conscience.[18]

Adherence to the Church's judgment and observance of the existing discipline concerning the obligation of canonical form necessary for the validity of the marriage of Catholics are what truly contribute to the spiritual welfare of the faithful concerned. The Church is in fact the body of Christ and to live in ecclesial communion is to live in the body of Christ and to nourish oneself with the body of Christ. With the reception of the sacrament of the Eucharist, communion with Christ the head can never be separated from communion with his members, that is, with his Church. For this reason, the sacrament of our union with Christ is also the sacrament of the unity of the Church. Receiving Eucharistic Communion contrary to the norms of ecclesial communion is therefore in itself a contradiction. Sacramental communion with Christ includes and presupposes the observance, even if at times difficult, of the order of ecclesial communion, and it cannot be right and fruitful if a member of the faithful, wishing to approach Christ directly, does not respect this order.

10. In keeping with what has been said above, the desire expressed by the Synod of Bishops, adopted by the Holy Father John Paul II as his own and put into practice with dedication and with praiseworthy initiatives by bishops, priests, religious and lay faithful is yet to be fully realized, namely, with solicitous charity to do everything that can be done to strengthen in the love of Christ and the Church those faithful in irregular marriage situations. Only thus will it be possible

for them fully to receive the message of Christian marriage and endure in faith the distress of their situation. In pastoral action one must do everything possible to ensure that this is understood not to be a matter of discrimination but only of absolute fidelity to the will of Christ who has restored and entrusted to us anew the indissolubility of marriage as a gift of the Creator. It will be necessary for pastors and the community of the faithful to suffer and to love in solidarity with the persons concerned so that they may recognize in their burden the sweet yoke and the light burden of Jesus.[19] Their burden is not sweet and light in the sense of being small or insignificant, but becomes light because the Lord—and with him the whole Church—shares it. It is the task of pastoral action, which has to be carried out with total dedication, to offer this help, founded in truth and in love together.

United with you in dedication to the collegial task of making the truth of Jesus Christ shine in the life and activity of the Church, I remain

Yours devotedly in the Lord,
Cardinal Joseph Ratzinger, prefect
Archbishop Alberto Bovone, secretary

During an audience granted to the cardinal prefect, the Supreme Pontiff John Paul II gave his approval to this letter, drawn up in the ordinary session of this congregation, and ordered its publication. Given at Rome, from the offices of the Congregation for the Doctrine of the Faith, Sept. 14, 1994, Feast of the Exaltation of the Holy Cross.

Notes

1. Cf. John Paul II, *Letter to Families* (Feb. 2, 1994), No. 3.
2. Cf. John Paul II, apostolic exhortation *Familiaris Consortio* (Nov. 22, 1981), Nos. 79–84: AAS 74 (1982) 180–186.
3. Cf. ibid., No. 84; *Letter to Families*, No. 5; *Catechism of the Catholic Church*, No. 1651.
4. Cf. Paul VI, encyclical letter *Humanae Vitae*, No. 29: AAS 60 (1968) 501; John Paul II, apostolic exhortation *Reconciliatio et Paenitentia*, No. 34: AAS 77 (1985) 272; encyclical letter *Veritatis Splendor*, No. 95: AAS 85 (1993) 1208.
5. Mark 10:11–12: "Whoever divorces his wife and marries another, commits adultery against her, and if she divorces her husband and marries another, she commits adultery."
6. Cf. *Catechism of the Catholic Church*, No. 1650; cf. also No. 1640 and the Council of Trent, sess. XXIV: DS 1797–1812.
7. *Familiaris Consortio*, No. 84.
8. Ibid, No. 84; cf. John Paul II, Homily on the Occasion of the Closure of the Sixth Synod of Bishops, No. 7: AAS 72 (1980) 1082.
9. *Familiaris Consortio*, No. 84.
10. Cf. 1 Cor. 11:27–29.
11. Cf. *Code of Canon Law*, 978.2.
12. Cf. *Catechism of the Catholic Church*, No. 1640.
13. Cf. Congregation for the Doctrine of the Faith, "Letter to the Bishops of the Catholic Church on Certain Questions Concerning the Minister of the Eucharist," III/4, AAS 75 (1983) 1007; St. Teresa of Avila, *The Way of Perfection*, 35, 1; St. Alphon-

sus de Liguori, *Visite al SS. Sacramento e a Maria Santissima.*

14. Cf. *Familiaris Consortio*, No. 84.
15. Cf. *Veritatis Splendor*, No. 55.
16. Cf. *Code of Canon Law*, 1085.2.
17. Cf. *Familiaris Consortio*, No. 84.
18. Cf. *Code of Canon Law*, 1536.2 and 1679 and *Code of the Canons of the Eastern Churches*, 1217.2 and 1365 concerning the probative force of the depositions of the parties in such processes.
19. Cf. Matt. 11:30.

Appendix 2

Apostolic Letter on Mixed Marriages: *Matrimonia Mixta*
Statement on the Implementation of the
Apostolic Letter on Mixed Marriages
By Pope Paul VI
October 1, 1970

Mixed marriages, that is to say marriages in which one party is a Catholic and the other a non-Catholic, whether baptized or not, have always been given careful attention by the Church in pursuance of her duty. Today the Church is constrained to give even greater attention to them, owing to the conditions of present times.

In the past, Catholics were separated from members of other Christian confessions and from non-Christians by their situation in their community or even by physical boundaries. In more recent times, however, not only has this separation been reduced, but communication between men of different regions and religions has greatly developed and, as a result, there has been a great increase in the number of mixed marriages.

Also, a great influence in this regard has been exercised by the growth and spread of civilization and industry, urbanization and consequent rural depopulation, migrations in great numbers and the increase in numbers of exiles of every kind.

The Church is indeed aware that mixed marriages, precisely because they admit differences of religion and are a consequence of the division among Christians, do not, except in some cases, help in reestablishing unity among Christians. There are many difficulties inherent in a mixed marriage, since a certain division is introduced into the living cell of the Church, as the Christian family is rightly called. And in the family itself the fulfillment of the Gospel teachings is more difficult because of diversities in matters of religion, especially with regard to those matters which concern Christian worship and the education of the children.

For these reasons the Church, conscious of her duty, discourages the contracting of mixed marriages, for she is the most desirous that Catholics be able in matrimony to attain to perfect union of mind and full communion of life. However, since man has the natural right to marry and beget children, the Church, by her laws, which clearly show her pastoral concern, makes such arrangements that on the one hand the principles of divine law be scrupulously observed and that on the other the said right to contract marriages be respected.

The Church vigilantly concerns herself with the education of the young and their fitness to undertake their duties with a sense of responsibility and to perform their obligations as members of the Church, and she shows this both in preparing for marriage those who intend to contract a mixed marriage and in caring for those who have already contracted such a marriage.

Although in the case of baptized persons of different religious confessions, there is less risk of religious indifferentism, it can be more easily avoided if both husband and wife have a sound knowledge of the Christian nature of marital partnership, and if they are properly helped by their respective Church authorities. Even difficulties arising in marriage between a Catholic and an unbaptized person can be overcome through pastoral watchfulness and skill.

Neither in doctrine nor in law does the Church place on the same level a marriage between a Catholic and a baptized non-Catholic, and one between a Catholic and an unbaptized person for, as the Second Vatican Council declared, men who, though they are not Catholics, "believe in Christ and have been properly baptized are brought into a certain, though imperfect, communion with the Catholic Church."[1] Moreover, although Eastern Christians who have been baptized outside the Catholic Church are separated from communion with us, they possess true sacraments, above all the priesthood and the Eucharist, whereby they are joined to us in a very close relationship.[2] Undoubtedly there exists in a marriage between baptized persons, since such a marriage is a true sacrament, a certain communion of spiritual benefits which is lacking in a marriage entered into by a baptized person and one who is not baptized.

Nevertheless, one cannot ignore the difficulties inherent even in mixed marriage between baptized persons. There is often a difference of opinion on the sacramental nature of matrimony, on the special significance of marriage celebrated within the Church, on the interpretation of certain moral principles pertaining to marriage and the family, on the extent to which obedience is due the Catholic Church, and on the competence that belongs to ecclesiastical authority. From this it is clear that difficult questions of this kind can only be resolved when Christian unity is restored.

The faithful must therefore be taught that, although the Church somewhat relaxes ecclesiastical discipline in particular cases, she can never remove the obligation of the Catholic party, which, by divine law, namely by the plan of salvation instituted through Christ, is imposed according to the various situations. The faithful should therefore be reminded that the Catholic party to a marriage has the duty of preserving his or her own faith. Nor is it ever permitted to expose oneself to a proximate danger of losing it. Furthermore, the Catholic partner in a mixed marriage is obliged, not only to remain steadfast in the faith, but also, as far as possible, to see to it that the children be baptized and brought up in that same faith and receive all those aids to eternal salvation which the Catholic Church provides for her sons and daughters.

The problem of the children's education is a particularly difficult one, in view of the fact that both husband and wife are bound by that responsibility and may by no means ignore it or any of the obligations connected with it. However, the Church endeavors to meet this problem, just as she does the others, by her legislation and pastoral care.

With all this in mind, no one will be really surprised to find that even the canonical discipline on mixed marriages cannot be uniform and that it must be adapted to the various cases in what pertains to the juridical form of contracting marriage, its liturgical celebration, and, finally, the pastoral care to be given to the married people, and the children of the marriage, according to the distinct circumstances of the married couple and the differing degrees of their ecclesiastical communion.

It was altogether fitting that so important a question should receive the attention of the Second Vatican Council. This occurred several times as occasion arose. Indeed, in the third session, the Council Fathers voted to entrust the question to us in its entirety. To meet their desire, the Sacred Congregation for the Doctrine of the Faith, on March 18, 1966, promulgated an instruction on mixed marriages, entitled *Matrimonii Sacramentum*,[3] which provided that, if the norms laid down therein stood the test of experience, they should be introduced in a definite and precise form into the Code of Canon Law which is now being revised.[4] When certain questions on mixed marriages were raised in the first general meeting of the Synod of Bishops, held in October, 1967,[5] and many useful observations had been made upon them by the Fathers, we decided to submit those questions to examination by a special commission of cardinals which, after diligent consideration, presented us with its conclusions.

At the outset we state that Eastern Catholics contracting marriage with baptized non-Catholics or with unbaptized persons are not subject to the norms established by this letter. With regard to the marriage of Catholics of whatsoever rite with Eastern, non-Catholic Christians, the Church has recently issued certain norms,[6] which we wish to remain in force.

Accordingly, in order that ecclesiastical discipline on mixed marriages be more perfectly formulated and that, without violating divine law, canon law should have regard for the differing circumstances of married couples, in accordance with the mind of the Second Vatican Council expressed especially in the decree *Unitatis Redintegratio*[7] and in the declaration *Dignitatis Humanae*,[8] and also in careful consideration of the wishes expressed in the Synod of Bishops, we, by our own authority, and after mature deliberation, establish and decree the following norms:

1. A marriage between two baptized persons, of whom one is a Catholic, while the other is a non-Catholic, may not licitly be contracted without the previous dispensation of the local ordinary [i.e., bishop of the local diocese], since such a marriage is by its nature an obstacle to the full spiritual communion of the married parties.

2. A marriage between two persons of whom one has been baptized in the Catholic Church or received into it, while the other is unbaptized, entered into without previous dispensation by the local ordinary, is invalid.

3. The Church, taking into account the nature and circumstances of times, places and persons, is prepared to dispense from both impediments, provided there is a just cause.

4. To obtain from the local ordinary dispensation from an impediment, the Catholic party shall declare that he is ready to remove dangers of falling from the faith. He is also gravely bound to make a sincere promise to do all in his power to have all the children baptized and brought up in the Catholic Church.

5. At an opportune time the non-Catholic party must be informed of these promises which the Catholic party has to make, so that it is clear that he is

cognizant of the promise and obligation on the part of the Catholic.

6. Both parties are to be clearly instructed on the ends and essential properties of marriage, not to be excluded by either party.

7. Within its own territorial competence, it is for the bishops' conference to determine the way in which these declarations and promises, which are always required, shall be made: whether by word of mouth alone, in writing, or before witnesses, and also to determine what proof of them there should be in the external forum, and how they are to be brought to the knowledge of the non-Catholic party, as well as to lay down whatever other requirements may be opportune.

8. The canonical form is to be used for contracting mixed marriages, and is required for validity, without prejudice, however, to the provisions of the decree *Crescens Matrimoniorum*, published by the Sacred Congregation for the Eastern Churches on February 22, 1967.[9]

9. If serious difficulties stand in the way of observing the canonical form, local Ordinaries have the right to dispense from the canonical form in any mixed marriage. But the bishops' conference is to determine norms according to which the said dispensation may be granted licitly and uniformly within the region or territory of the conference, with the provision that there should always be some public form of ceremony.

10. Arrangements must be made that all validly contracted marriages be diligently entered in the books prescribed by canon law. Priests responsible should make sure that non-Catholic ministers also assist in recording in their books the fact of

a marriage with a Catholic. Episcopal conferences are to issue regulations determining, for their region or territory, a uniform method by which a marriage that has been publicly contracted after a dispensation from the canonical form was obtained, is registered in the books prescribed by canon law.

11. With regard to the liturgical form of the celebration of a mixed marriage, if it is to be taken from the Roman ritual, use must be made of the ceremonies in the rite of celebration of marriage promulgated by our authority, whether it is a question of a marriage between a Catholic and a baptized non-Catholic (39–54) or of a marriage between a Catholic and an unbaptized person (55–66). If, however, the circumstances justify it, a marriage between a Catholic and a baptized non-Catholic can be celebrated, subject to the local ordinary's consent, according to the rites for the celebration of marriage within Mass (19–38), while respecting the prescription of general law with regard to Eucharistic communion.

12. The episcopal conferences shall inform the Apostolic See of all decisions which, within their competence, they make concerning mixed marriages.

13. The celebration of marriage before a Catholic priest or deacon and a non-Catholic minister, performing their respective rites together, is forbidden. Nor is it permitted to have another religious marriage ceremony before or after the Catholic ceremony, for the purpose of giving or renewing matrimonial consent.

14. Local ordinaries and parish priests shall see to it that the Catholic husband or wife and the children born of a mixed marriage do not lack spiritual

assistance in fulfilling their duties of conscience. They shall encourage the Catholic husband or wife to keep ever in mind the divine gift of the Catholic faith and to bear witness to it in gentleness and reverence, and with a clear conscience.[10] They are to aid the married couple to foster the unity of their conjugal and family life, a unity which, in the case of Christians, is based on their baptism too. To these ends it is to be desired that those pastors should establish relationships of sincere openness and enlightened confidence with ministers of other religious communities.

15. The penalties decreed by canon 2319[*] of the Code of Canon Law are all abrogated. For those who have already incurred them the effects of those penalties cease, without prejudice to the obligations mentioned in number 4 of these norms.

16. The local ordinary is able to give a *"sanatio in radice"* of a mixed marriage, when the conditions spoken of in numbers 4 and 5 of these norms have been fulfilled, and provided that the conditions of the law are observed.

17. In case of a particular difficulty or doubt with regard to the application of these norms, recourse is to be made to the Holy See. We order that what we have decreed in this letter, given in the form of *"motu proprio,"* be regarded as established and

---

[*] Canon 2319, 1: "Catholics are under an excommunication latae sententiae reserved to the ordinary: (1) who contract marriage before a non-Catholic minister contrary to canon 1063, 51, 1; (2) who contract marriage with an explicit or implicit agreement that all children or any child be educated outside the Catholic Church; (3) who knowingly presume to present their children to non-Catholic ministers to be baptized; (4) who, being parents or taking their place, knowingly present their children to be educated or trained in a non-Catholic religion.

ratified, notwithstanding any measure to the contrary, and is to take effect from the first day of October of this year (1970).

Notes

1. Decree on Ecumenism, *Unitatis Redintegratio*, 3, AAS 57 (1965), p. 93. Cf. Dogmatic Constitution on the Church, *Lumen Gentium*, AAS 57 (1965), pp. 19-20.
2. Cf. Second Vatican Council: Decree on Ecumenism, *Unitatis Redintegratio*, 13-18, l.c., pp. 100-104.
3. Cf. AAS 58 (1966), pp. 235-239.
4. Cf. ibid. l.c., p. 237.
5. Cf. *Argumenta de quibus disceptabitur in primo generali coetu Synodi Episcoporum, pars altera, Typis Polyglottis Vaticanis*, 1967, pp. 27-37.
6. Cf. Second Vatican Council: "Decree on Eastern Catholic Churches," *Orientalium Ecclesiarum*, 18, AAS 57 (1965), p. 82, Sacred Congregation for the Eastern Churches: Decree *Crescens Matrimoniorum*, AAS 59 (1967), pp. 165-166.
7. AAS 57 (1965), pp. 90-112.
8. AAS 58 (1966), pp. 929-946.
9. Cf. AAS 59 (1967), p. 166.
10. Cf. 1 Peter 3:16.

Appendix 3

Sacred Congregation for the Doctrine of the Faith
Instruction on Mixed Marriages: *Matrimonii Sacramentum*

That the Sacrament of Matrimony, established by Christ as a sign of His union with the Church, may fully exert its sacred power and really be for the spouses a great mystery (Eph. 5:32) by which they in the intimate union of their life symbolize the love by which Christ gave Himself for men, there is the greatest demand for full and perfect harmony of the spouses especially, in matters pertaining to religion "for union of minds is wont to be severed, or at least weakened, where the highest and most important matters which man holds sacred, that is, in religious truths and convictions, there arises a difference of opinion and disagreement of purpose" (Pius XI, Encyclical Letter: *Casti Connubii*). Therefore, the Catholic Church considers it her most serious duty to safeguard and protect the welfare of the faith both in the spouses and in the children. Consequently the Church strives with the greatest care and vigilance that Catholics contract marriage with Catholics.

Now the clear proof of this unremitting vigilance is the Church's discipline in regard to mixed marriages sanctioned the prescriptions of the Code of Canon Law which is expressed in the form of a twofold impediment namely of mixed religion and disparity of cult. Of these the first forbids the marriage of Catholics with baptized non-Catholics, the validity of this marriage, however, being intact (Canons 1060–1064). The other renders invalid the marriage contracted by a Catholic with a non-baptized person (Canons 1070–1071).

Another proof of this concern of the Church to safeguard the sanctity of Christian marriage is the juridical form itself of expressing consent. Although in the past there have been diverse norms concerning the form, nevertheless care has always been taken that clandestine marriages were not permitted.

Following this course let all the Shepherds teach the faithful the religious importance and value of this Sacrament. Let them gravely warn the faithful of the difficulties and dangers which are inherent in contracting a marriage with a Christian non-Catholic, and much more with a non-Christian. By all suitable means let them bring it about that young people contract marriage with a Catholic party.

It must nevertheless be admitted that the peculiar conditions of our age which in a short time have brought such important changes into social and family life, have made the observance of the canonical discipline in regard to mixed marriages more difficult than in times past. Under these circumstances it now happens that communications, acquaintances, and contacts of Catholics with non-Catholics are more frequent, and so the bonds of friendship are more easily established between them which, as is evident from experience, are wont to bring on more frequent occasions of mixed marriages.

Accordingly, the pastoral solicitude of the Church today even more demands that in mixed marriages also the sanctity of matrimony in keeping with Catholic teaching, and the faith of the Catholic spouse be completely safeguarded and that the Catholic education of the children be cared for with the greatest possible diligence and effectiveness. This pastoral care is therefore more necessary because, as is known, there are found among non-Catholics diverse opinions both concerning the essence of marriage and its qualities, especially in regard to indissolubility and consequently about divorce and contracting marriage after divorce (civil). The Church therefore considers it her duty to protect her faithful that they may not endanger the faith and suffer harm either spiritual or material. Therefore, those who intend to contract marriage are to be instructed accurately about the nature, qualities, and obligations of matrimony and the dangers that must he avoided.

Moreover, in this matter, the course of conduct of Catholics now to be observed with brethren separated from the Catholic Church as it was solemnly established by the Second Ecumenical Council of the Vatican through the "Decree on Ecumenism" is not to be forgotten.

This decree seems to suggest that the rigor of the current discipline concerning mixed marriages be mitigated, not indeed in those matters which pertain to divine law, but in some norms introduced by ecclesiastical law by which the separated brethren not infrequently think they are being offended.

It can easily be inferred that a most serious question of this kind in no way escaped the notice of the

Second Ecumenical Council of the Vatican which was summoned by our predecessor of happy memory, Pope John XXIII, for the very purpose of providing for today's needs of the Christian people. And as a matter of fact the Council Fathers set forth various opinions in this matter which indeed, as was fitting, have been carefully considered.

Therefore, after joint consultation with the sacred Shepherds whom it concerns, all matters having been duly weighed, with the two impediments of mixed religion and disparity of cult remaining in force-local Ordinaries, however, having been granted according to the Apostolic Letter *Pastorale munus*, numbers 19 and 20, the power to dispense from these impediments when grave causes exist and when the requirements of law have been observed-the law of the Eastern Churches remaining intact, the following provisions are established by the authority of Pope Paul VI, and if verified by experience they will be inserted in a fixed and definitive way in the Code of Canon Law which is now being revised.

I.

1. It should always be kept in mind that danger to the faith is to be warded off from the Catholic spouse and that the education of the child in the Catholic religion must be cared for diligently (cf. Canon 1060).

2. The local ordinary or the pastor of the Catholic party will take care to inculcate in grave words the obligation of always providing for the baptism and education of the future offspring in the Catholic religion. The fulfillment of this obligation will

be assured by the explicit promise or guarantee made by the same Catholic party.

3. The non-Catholic party with due respect, but in a clear manner, is certainly to be informed of the Catholic teaching about the dignity of matrimony and especially about its chief qualities which are unity and indissolubility. The grave obligation of the Catholic spouse to guard, preserve, profess his (her) own faith and to baptize and educate in that faith the offspring that may be born must be made known to the same non-Catholic party. Since this obligation must be safeguarded, the non-Catholic entering marriage is to be invited to promise sincerely and openly that he will in no way impede this obligation. If, however, the non-Catholic party thinks that he cannot make this promise without violating his own conscience, the ordinary is to refer the case with all its circumstances to the Holy See.

4. Although by the ordinary law these promises are to be given in writing, it is, however, in the power of the ordinary to decide, either in general or in individual cases, whether this promise of the Catholic party or the non-Catholic party or of both is to be given in writing or not, and likewise to determine how this is to be entered in the marriage records.

II.

If in some place, as sometimes happens in some regions, the Catholic education of the child is prevented not so much by the choice of the spouses as by the laws and customs of the people which those entering marriage are forced to obey, the local ordinary, when everything is carefully considered, can dispense from this impediment, provided that the Catholic party is ready, in so far as he knows and is able, to do everything that every child that will be born be baptized and educated as a Catholic and that there is certainty of the good will of the non-Catholic party. In making these concessions, the Church is led by the hope that the civil laws contrary to human liberty, such as those which forbid the Catholic education of the child or the practice of the Catholic religion, will be abolished and that the natural law will prevail in these matters.

III.

In celebrating mixed marriages the canonical form which is dealt with in Canon 1094 must be observed and indeed for validity. If, however, difficulties arise, the ordinary shall refer the case with its circumstances to the Holy See.

IV.

As far as the liturgical form is concerned, by derogating canons 1102, paragraph 2, and 1109, paragraph 3, power is granted to the local ordinaries to permit the celebration of mixed marriages also with the use of sacred rites and the customary blessings and the sermon.

V.

Any celebration of a marriage before a Catholic priest and a non-Catholic minister in which each one simultaneously carries out his own rite must be avoided absolutely. Nevertheless, there is no objection that the non-Catholic minister speak some words of congratulation and exhortation after the religious ceremony is concluded, and that some prayers be recited with the non-Catholics. All this may be done with the approval of the local ordinary and the use of timely precautions to avoid the danger of astonishment.

VI.

Local ordinaries and pastors shall be diligently watchful that the families which grow from mixed marriages live conscientiously according to the promises that have been made, especially in regard to imbuing the offspring with Catholic teaching and morals.

VII.

The excommunication, with which according to Canon 2319, paragraph 1, number 1, those are penalized who contract marriage before a non-Catholic minister, is abrogated. The effects of this abrogation are retroactive.

These norms are established with that mind and the intention which we have disclosed above: to make fuller provisions for the current needs of the faithful, and that the mutual relations between Catholics and non-Catholics be influenced by a greater feeling of charity.

Wholeheartedly, therefore, and with constant attention, let those who discharge the office of imparting Catholic teaching to the faithful devote themselves to this task, especially the pastors. Let them strive to carry out this task by employing the greatest charity toward the faithful and always without prejudice to due regard for others, namely non-Catholics and also to their persuasions, based on good faith. Let Catholic spouses, however, take care to strengthen and increase in themselves the gift of faith, and ever following the paths of Christian virtues in their family life let them also continually give the non-Catholic party and their children a shining example.

> Given at Rome on the eighteenth day of
> March in the year 1966
> A. Cardinal Ottaviani, Pro-Prefect
> Peter Parente, Secretary

Glossary of Major Terms

Affirmative A short-hand way of saying that an annulment was granted. Derived from the fact that the *dubia* was answered in the affirmative, that is, the nullity of the marriage was proved. Sometimes called a *constat* (it is proven).

Annulment A common term for what is more accurately called a declaration of matrimonial nullity, an official determination that what appeared to be a valid marriage was not one. Not a divorce.

Assessor An advisor to a judge, not necessarily degreed in canon law but usually very knowledgeable in canon law, can be either a cleric or layperson

Auditor A tribunal official, cleric or lay, often but not necessarily degreed in canon law, who assists in the investigation of a case. Auditors generally have the same authority as judges in gathering evidence in a case, but they do not make the final decision.

Canon A specific, numbered, provision of canon law.

Canon Law The internal legal system of the Catholic Church, and the main body of ecclesiastical rules under which annulment cases are heard. Most of canon law is found in the Code of Canon Law.

Citation Usually refers to the official notice given by the tribunal to the respondent that a marriage is being impugned by the petitioner. Sometimes refers also to the notice sent to witnesses that their cooperation is being requested.

Civil marriage Marriage recognized by civil law, but not necessarily by canon law. The civil marriages of non-Catholics are usually presumed valid. The term is also used to describe an attempt at marriage made by Catholics without observing canonical form.

Code of Canon Law The one volume book which contains the complete text of the 1,752 individual canons of Church law. Most recently issued for Roman Catholics in 1983.

Competence, Tribunal Canonical authority to hear a case, basically the same as jurisdiction.

Consent The commitment of a person capable of marriage, given in accord with canonical form, to marriage as the Church understands and proclaims it.

Convalidation Popularly termed "having a marriage blessed in the Church," a convalidation is the renewal of consent necessary before a marriage can be recognized as valid if that marriage was entered into despite the presence of a nondispensed impediment, or with insufficient consent to marriage as the Church understands and proclaims it, or in violation of canonical form.

Declaration of Nullity Also, declaration of matrimonial nullity or annulment. The decision by a diocesan tribunal or other qualified canonical court that what appeared to be, from one or more points of view, a valid marriage, was not one.

Dubium, Dubia An official Latin term that means a doubt about the validity of the impugned marriage.

Form Also, canonical form, the actual process by which a Catholic marries in the Church. Often does, but need not, take place during a wedding Mass.

Impediment Certain qualities, recognized under canon law, which, if present at the time of the wedding, render the person canonically incapable of entering valid marriage, despite good intentions and the observance of canonical form, if that was required.

Impugned Canonically questioned or put up for review; a marriage that is being officially investigated for possible nullity is being impugned.

Instance A tribunal or ecclesiastical court; also, the trial heard in such courts. There are always two, and sometimes three, instances in affirmative annulment cases.

Licit Done in accord with Church rules. Although most things in Church life which are done licitly are also done validly, a wedding can be licit, but still be found invalid.

Marriage A permanent, exclusive relationship between a man and woman which is ordered toward the good of the spouses and the procreation and education of children. The marriages of two baptized (but not necessarily Catholic) persons are also sacramental.

Monitum A Latin term meaning a suggestion, but not an order, by a bishop or by the tribunal that a person take certain steps before attempting another marriage in the Church, even though an annulment has already declared him or her free to marry in the Church.

Negative A short-hand way of saying an annulment was not granted. Derived from the fact that the *dubia* was answered in the negative, that is, nullity was not proved. Sometimes called a *non constat* (it is not proven).

Null Something which, even despite appearances to the contrary, was of no force from its beginning.

Parties The petitioner and the respondent in an annulment case, the former spouses of the marriage.

Petition Also *libellus* (little book), the documents submitted by the petitioner in which the petitioner's request for an annulment is presented.

Petitioner The person who files for an annulment. The petitioner can be either the husband or the wife. In some cases, the Promoter of Justice can file an annulment case.

Prohibition An order sometimes placed on either or both parties to a null marriage which, despite the granting of the annulment, forbids remarriage in the Church until certain conditions are satisfied. Sometimes called *vetitum* (prohibition).

Radical Sanation Much like a convalidation, but not requiring a renewal of consent. Not used often.

Renunciation Withdrawing a nullity petition before it is adjudicated.

Respondent The other spouse in an annulment case, the one who is asked to respond to the filing of an annulment.

Tribunal A panel of one or three canonical judges, appointed to office by the diocesan bishop, which decides whether canonical cases like annulments have been filed and proven in accord with canon law.

Valid Canonically binding and requiring respect by the Church. Not necessarily licit, but juridically effective in its goal.

Index

Index of Canons Cited

About the Author

Dr. Edward N. Peters received his civil law degree from the University of Missouri at Columbia and his doctoral degree in canon law from the Catholic University of America. He has held a number of teaching and administrative posts, and presently serves as Director of the Office for Canonical Affairs for the Diocese of San Diego as well as collegiate judge on the diocesan and appellate tribunal. His articles and reviews have appeared in a wide variety of Catholic and secular publications and he is a consultant to many ecclesiastical institutions and persons. He and his wife Angela are raising six children.